40 DAYS to Soul Expansion

A GUIDED JOURNEY OF Self-Discovery AND Truth

Tearlisa Wilder

For permission requests, write to the publisher, addressed "Attention: Permissions Coordinator," at the address below, or by e-mail at thesoulsharmony@yahoo.com.

Tearhsa D Wilder
P.O. Box 15328
Surfside Beach, SC 29587

ISBN-13: 978-0-692-95049-4
ISBN-10: 0-692-95049-4

Cover and layout design: Rachel Dunham and Heather McNamara, www.YourBrandTherapy.com

Editor: Bryna Haynes, www.TheHeartOfWriting.com

Printed in the United States of America

Dedication

This collection of personal growth lessons is
dedicated to everyone who has committed to
undertake a shift of consciousness in our world.
As we grow personally, we grow collectively.

Praise

As the reader embarks on the journey of "40 Days to Soul Expansion", the possibilities of self-discovery are limitless! This book provides a powerful opportunity of a lifetime. Enjoy!

DR. CAROL MCCALL, PHD, MCC.,
Founder, The Institute for Global Listening and Communication, LLC

Tearhsa has inspired yet another 40 days of soul awakening! Sharing the possibilities for self-love, illumination, reflection, and mastery, she has gifted you with creative, mindful, simple and powerful practices for being present to all that is and all that you are. Beautiful….simply and profoundly beautiful!

TUCK,
The Rebel Belle

In her new book, Tearhsa gives us a perfect tool for doing our inner work. Most of us have tried 'filling up' through the outer, but realized it doesn't cut it. We have known we needed to turn inward for finding ourselves and we needed a roadmap. Thank you Tearhsa for helping us all on our path.

JEAN ADRIENNE,
Developer of InnerSpeak, Author

Preface

In May 2017, I felt a welling of energy flowing in and around my being. The flow of communication from my guidance became centered and powerful. I felt elevated to a space of intense love, focus and connection.

Right away, I knew there was a message to be revealed. With pencil in hand, I asked, "What am I being called to?" As the messages began to pour in, once again I found that my pencil cannot move as quickly as my intuitive reception. However, the core of the message was that I was to use my prior writings from my book, 40 Days to Soul Enlightenment, as a guideline to create a program for continued soul expansion.

Using the titles from each day of 40 Days to Soul Enlightenment as I was guided, I began with Day 1 — Mindfulness, and asked, "What is the soul expansion message I am to relay?" I wrote and wrote. With each daily bit of insightful information came an action. These actions took the form of a worksheet to accompany each daily lesson.

I isolated myself and wrote manically for three weeks. I was exhausted, yet vibrant simultaneously. It was a beautiful experience. After each writing session and each download of the worksheet information, I found myself with a fullness within my heart, a joy throughout my soul and a big smile on my face. At times, I just shook my head in wonderment.

I am so very honored to be chosen as the conduit of these messages. The growth I received throughout the manifestation of this collection has been ... well, there are no words to describe this journey. I know myself so much more intimately than I did before. I know how I relate in this life and to this life. I know where and how I serve. I am in deep relation with myself my guidance, all creation and most importantly, "I AM".

Much love and many blessings on your journey to soul expansion.

Tearhga

A note on the language in this book:

In these pages, you will find many references to "God". This is common language for me. Some of you may find this name or reference uncomfortable; some will not. Regardless of your personal beliefs, remember that we all serve a higher power. I choose to address this Source as "God". You can use any label or term that feels good to you. We are all connected as one in this Universe and the Creator, Source, Divine and Higher Self are one and the same. Ultimately, my goal is not to show you God as I see him, but to show you your highest power as He/She/It sees you.

"How to use this book:"

40 Days to Soul Expansion is a self-paced program designed to bring you closer to knowledge and truth through information and action. The goal is to expand your open heart and heighten awareness of your true self.

The program consists of forty separate lessons. Each is comprised of a daily affirmation, information and a worksheet—all the pieces you need to have an integrated, expansive daily experience.

We each have our unique experiences and design; therefore, it may take you a bit longer than forty days to complete these exercises based on your individual goals and healing process. Allow yourself the time you need to process, release and heal after each day's work before moving forward. As you feel the inner shift, you will know you are ready to continue.

I suggest creating a separate notebook for journaling your thoughts and personal progress. Before starting each lesson, set aside uninterrupted "me time". Have your worksheets and journal available prior to beginning the exercises.

There are 10 free audio downloads included to guide you through the meditations and visualizations. Type the link in to your browser and follow the prompts. *https://thesoulsharmony.com/40-day-soul-expansion-download/*

Each day also has a daily affirmation. Write the affirmation down and carry it with you throughout the whole time you are working that lesson. Read it regularly and post it in multiple locations such as on your bathroom mirror, the dashboard of your car, your desk or the refrigerator.

Most of all, remember that this program is about you and no one else. Dedicate yourself to yourself. You are worth it!

Many Blessings,

Tearhsa

Audio Meditations & Visualizations

To listen to the audio meditations in this book, go to:

https://thesoulsharmony.com/40-day-soul-expansion-download/

DAY 2 – RECOGNITION

DAY 3 – OBSERVATION

DAY 4 – AWARENESS

DAY 5 – I AM A CHILD OF GOD

DAY 20 – INTO THE LIGHT

DAY 29 – THE HEART – WITH THE HEART BLESSING ATTUNEMENT

DAY 33 – LIFE REVIEW

DAY 38 – HEALING INTENTIONS

DAY 39 – FAITH & REFLECTION OF GOD

Background music from Orin & DaBen:

https://www.orindaben.com/

Technical Contributor, Hilarie Cox,

heartmindconsulting.com

Contents

40 DAYS to Soul Expansion

DAY ONE

Mindfulness

Affirmation:

"On this day, I connect on a soul level with all creation."

Spend today being mindful of all creation. By doing this, you can learn to view yourself and all that surrounds you with an open heart and a deeper understanding. By taking time to connect on a soul level with everything around you and ponder the meaning in every encounter, you can embrace all of life; you can understand the purpose of each breath, moment and being. You will then find gratitude for all.

Throughout your day, take time to pause. Notice the air you breathe, the ground beneath your feet, the breeze on your skin, the feel of the sun/rain/chill in the air. Pause and turn in place, slowly revolving three hundred sixty degrees as you take in all that surrounds you; look at every living and inanimate object, respecting the existence and purpose of each. Communicate with each, recognizing the beauty within each piece of grass, each tree. If you are sitting in your office, notice the items on your desk, the structure of the building, the busyness of the people around you.

No matter where you are, you can find beauty, for beauty does lie within all existence.

Pause at least four times today. Pay particular attention to how you feel each time and your emotions as you view each part of your surroundings. Journal your feelings on your worksheet.

Also, as you encounter others in all settings—at home, work, the gym, school, restaurants or the grocery store—look at each person before you with your loving heart. Feel their presence on a deeper level of kindness, love, appreciation. See them as the wonder they are. Connect heart to heart. See a stream of light from your heart to theirs. Know that each encounter holds meaning and reason and each holds an opportunity for a lesson. Even brief encounters may hold the gift of love as you exchange energy and share this reality together.

Practice leaving each person with happiness and uplifted energy. As you part, notice your feelings and emotions without attachment. Place no judgement around the encounter as "positive" or "negative". Even unpleasant encounters are opportunities for growth. Instead, observe, respect and note the purpose of each encounter and the events surrounding it. All serves a purpose.

Journal your thoughts on your worksheet.

Worksheet

Pause 4-5 times today to breathe and fully embrace the environment around you. Turn 360° slowly. Take in everything in your view. Notice the function, design and purpose of each. Do you have an attachment or connection?

After each observation, journal what you noticed and any thoughts that arose.

1ST OBSERVATION

2ND OBSERVATION

3RD OBSERVATION

4TH OBSERVATION

5TH OBSERVATION

Connect with each person you encounter heart to heart. See a stream of light from your heart to theirs. Feel their presence on a deep level. Observe your feelings and emotions without attachment.

What is the true purpose of the encounter and the events surrounding it?

NAME

FEELING/EMOTION

PURPOSE

NAME

FEELING/EMOTION

PURPOSE

NAME

FEELING/EMOTION

PURPOSE

NAME

FEELING/EMOTION

PURPOSE

NAME

FEELING/EMOTION

PURPOSE

NAME

FEELING/EMOTION

PURPOSE

NAME

FEELING/EMOTION

PURPOSE

NAME

FEELING/EMOTION

PURPOSE

NAME

FEELING/EMOTION

PURPOSE

DAY TWO

Recognition

Affirmation:

"On this day, I am open to the wisdom of life."

Recognition of self and environment heightens awareness and respect for creation.

By taking notice of all things individually and collectively, and thus recognizing the makeup and contribution of your reality, you can begin to understand and appreciate the world you live in. Practicing recognition will assist in cultivating appreciation and gratitude and with bringing into life those things which bring joy.

Find a quiet place to sit comfortably for this visualization session. Engage with the audio recording*, or guide yourself through this reflection.

Meditation

Recognition Meditation

Close your eyes and imagine standing in the middle of the ocean on top of the water. Feel the breeze in your hair, the sun on your skin, the splash of the waves. Imagine the many life forms below you–their shapes, sizes and purpose in the eco balance. Breathe in this magnificence.

Now, take yourself to the mountains. As you stand amongst the tall, tall trees, listen to the sounds of the forest: leaves rustling in the wind, the scurry of small animals amongst the brush and bark. Feel the calm around you. Notice your feelings as you become one with nature.

Now, move (in your imagination) to a nearby park. Sit on the cool grass. Connect with Mother Earth, listen to the laughter of children playing and hear the rhythm of the bicycles passing by. Feel the joy deep within as you become one with a passing butterfly. Lie back on the grass, close your eyes and take in the beauty and life surrounding you.

Next, move to a city street. Observe the hustle and bustle as people pass you by, each with their different agendas, thoughts, aspirations, joys and pains. Feel the sidewalk below your feet, the structures that surround you. Notice the multitude of textures. Hear the mumble of conversation, the cars driving by and the sounds of construction in the background. Focus your attention on each, then collectively as they come together to form this perfect moment.

Move now to your own home. Imagine yourself sitting in your living room. What does the couch or chair feel like under you? Picture each item around you: the pillows, the table, TV, the overhead light; picture the window that brings the outside in. Look at the various personal items in the room that reflect your character. Do you see yourself represented in this space? Does every color, curtain, furnishing and decoration speak to you? Lean back in your seat as you relax into your personal space and feel the safety, comfort and familiarity of your home.

Focus now upon yourself. Tune in to each of your body parts: your toes, feet, legs, fingers, arms, torso, neck, head and face. Notice how each part functions and reacts to the others. Notice how your thoughts power these actions—how some, like breathing, are automatic, and others, such as raising your arm, require conscious focus. The intricacy of the human body is endless. Relax into the rhythm of your heartbeat and explore your body.

Bring your awareness back into your body now, slowly moving your extremities. Then, open your eyes.

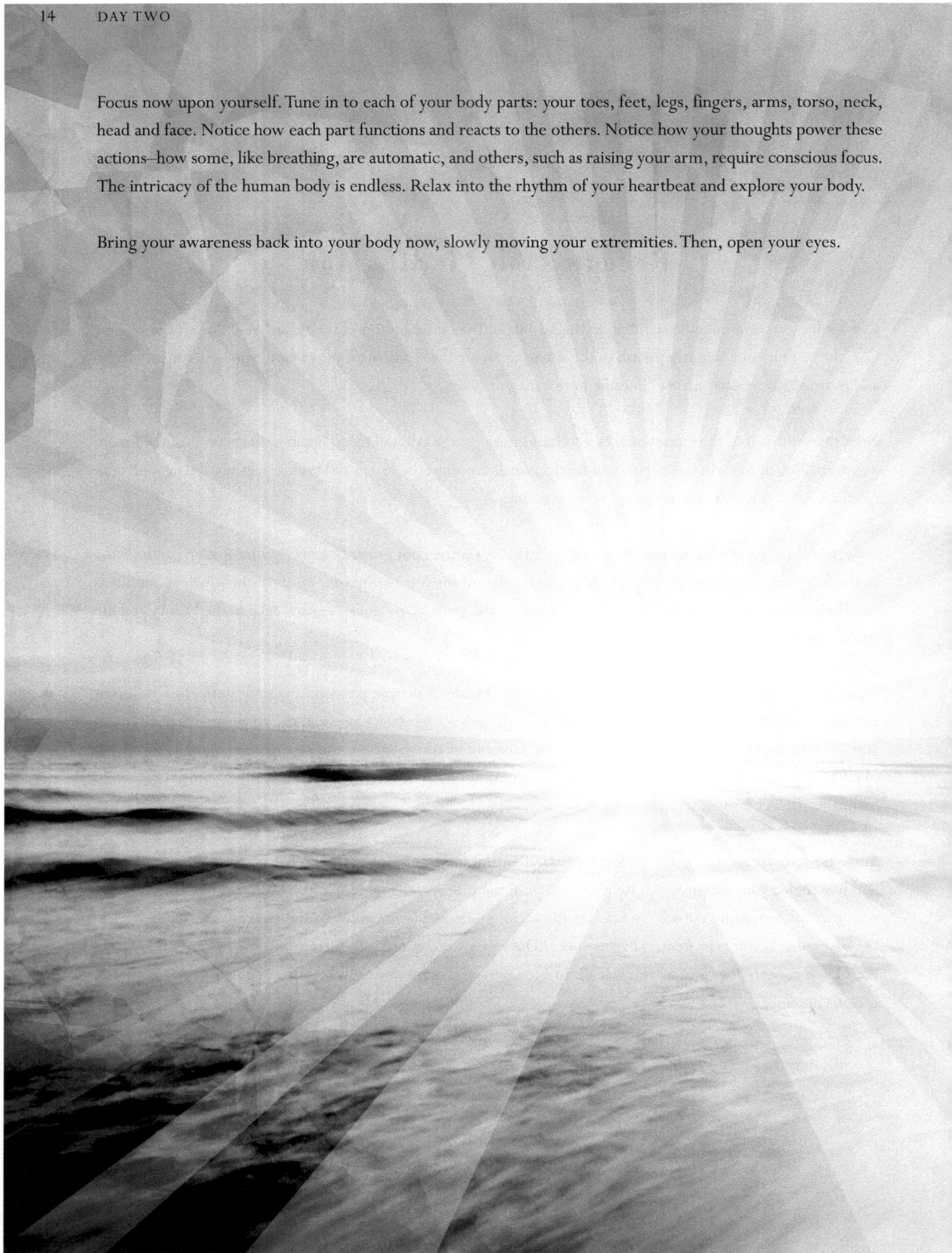

Worksheet

For each segment of the visualization, answer the questions below.

1. What stood out most to you?

_____

_____

_____

_____

_____

2. What was your level of comfort (1 = extremely comfortable, 10 = anxious)

○   ○   ○   ○   ○   ○   ○   ○   ○   ○
1   2   3   4   5   6   7   8   9   10

3. Did you feel a special connection with anything particular?

_____

_____

_____

_____

_____

4. Did you feel the connectivity and balance in each environment/space?

_____

_____

_____

_____

_____

_____

5. Did you find value in both the small, individual parts and the combined?

_____

_____

_____

_____

_____

OCEAN

_____

_____

_____

MOUNTAINS

PARK

CITY STREET

HOME

YOURSELF

DAY THREE

Observation

Affirmation:

On this day, I merge with the energies of the Sun and Moon."

Begin by placing your focus upon your heart. Feel each heartbeat as it pulses through your body.

Today you will immerse yourself in the great outdoors during the day to observe the sun and at night to observe the moon. In between, pause at every opportunity and look up, noticing the location of the sun and the moon as they travel across the sky. This will assist you in connecting with both.

Observe the sun and the moon: feel the magnitude of each and honor the force that each brings forth. Become aware of the life around you and how it is nourished and strengthened through placement. Feel the pull between yourself and the sun, and yourself and the moon.

The following meditations are to assist with your observations. Engage with the audio recording* or guide yourself through each.

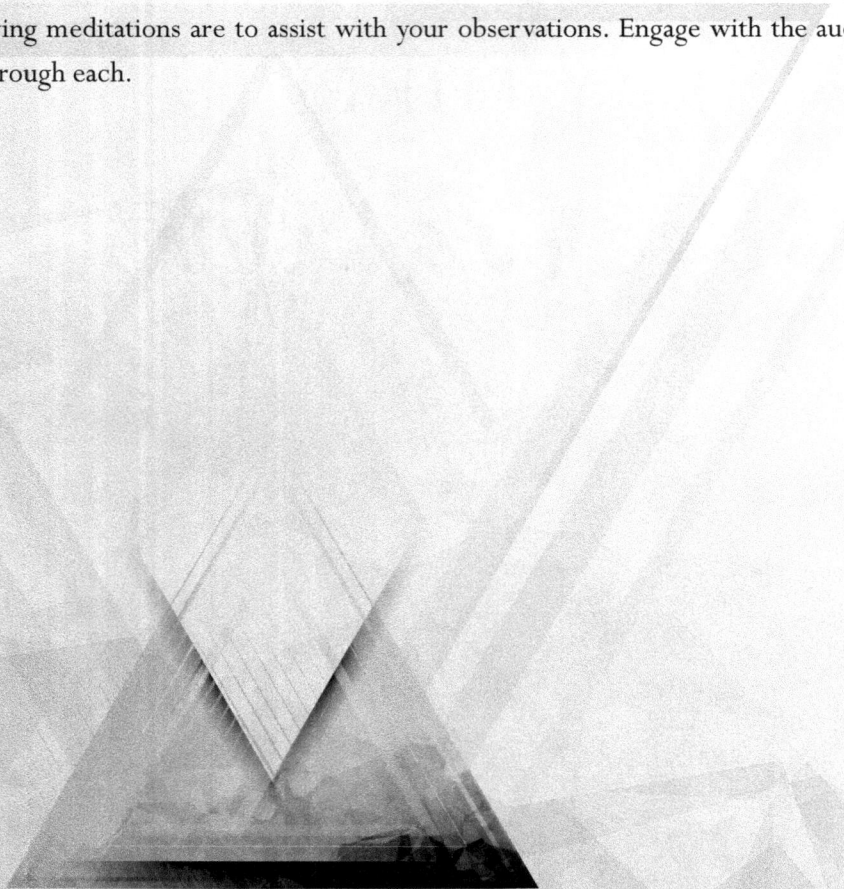

Meditation

Observation Meditation

SUN SEGMENT

Sitting comfortably in full sunlight, notice the sun and its location. Feel the rays as they penetrate your skin and the earth's surface. It is warm or hot?

Imagine the distance between you and the sun. Feel the healing energies. Now place your awareness on the ground in front of you. How does the sun nurture the grass, the soil, the trees and flowers? Notice how each bit of nature relies on the suns' rays for growth, health and sustenance.

Now broaden your view to include your neighborhood, your town, your state, your continent. Continue to broaden your thoughts as you see the sun in relation to Mother Earth. Observe the sun as it offers its' nurturing love to all living things. The sun's love provides for you.

MOON SEGMENT

As you bask in the moonlight, begin to feel the moon's energetic pull in and around you. Relax into its comforting energy. How do you feel? Calm? Free?

Gazing upon the moon, notice the shape. Is it a new moon? Full moon? First or last quarter? Is the moon eclipsed? Notice the moon's aura: is it close or widespread? What colors do you see—white, gold or the full spectrum of the rainbow?

Now, close your eyes as you deeply connect with the moon and its offering. Connect deeper and deeper. Bringing your awareness to your heart center, begin expanding that moon energy until you are completely surrounded in the glowing magnitude of the moon's pulsating, delightful hug. Continue to receive the moon's gifts to you.

Bringing your awareness back to your surroundings, see all within your view. Then, imagine beyond your view to all of Earth's existence. Know that you are one with all and that the moon's gift is expansive, given freely to all.

Worksheet

Journal your experience from your time with the sun and the moon.

Did you feel the connection and the energies within yourself?

How did the energies feel different from one another?

How does the sun nurture you, the earth and life? How does the moon nurture you, the earth, and life?

SUN

MOON

ADDITIONAL NOTES

DAY FOUR

Awareness

Affirmation:

"On this day, I harmonize with nature."

Perform this meditation in a quiet place in nature. Engage with the audio recording* or guide yourself through this reflection.

---

*You can download an audio version of this guided meditation at https://thesoulsharmony.com/40-Day-Soul-Expansion-Download/

Meditation

Awareness Meditation

As you sit comfortably in nature, begin to observe all that surrounds you—the grass, the earth, the trees, the sky and the tiny little insects scurrying around. See the birds, butterflies and flowers. Perhaps there is water nearby, filled with fish, frogs and plants.

Pick one of these life forms to focus on. What brings it nourishment? The soil, the sun, the rain? Is it dependent upon others to bring it nourishment? What does it contribute to the environment? How does it survive? How is it fed?

Now, bring your awareness to your heart center. With each breath, feel your heart opening. Picturing a white beam of light from your heart, send that light to the living organism of your choice—the butterfly, the grass, the tree, whichever you chose. Connecting with that organism, begin to feel its presence and imagine that you are that organism. What do you feel? Are you small and looking up? Large and looking down? Free to travel or steadfast? What can you see from your point of view? What nourishes you and brings you joy?

Backing up now, bring your awareness back to self. Then, choose something completely opposite to connect with. For example, if you chose a tree before, focus on an animal and vice versa. Open your heart once again, expanding with each breath. Send your heart light out to connect. Become one with the organism of your choice and evaluate your thoughts, emotions and needs as you commune with this living organism.

Bring your focus back upon your heart center once again. Now, apply this same heart connection and observation to your own self, your own needs. What nourishes you? What brings you joy? Are you large or small, stationary or mobile? Notice the string of effect from yourself to all that surrounds you.

With yourself included, see Earth and all its life with the understanding that we are all dependent upon one another. Each of us has special needs of varying types. We are similar, yet different; all are connected to bring balance. The balance of life must be managed in order to sustain.

Know that surrounding each organism, assigned to every living creature, are special watchkeepers. These are specialists that know and assist with needs and connection. By honoring yourself and all that you are connected to, you honor each of the special watchkeepers that bring beauty, joy and harmony to the world you have been given.

Worksheet

Record your thoughts below

1ST ORGANISM

2ND ORGANISM

AWARENESS OF SELF

AWARENESS OF BALANCE

ADDITIONAL NOTES

34

DAY FIVE

I Am A Child of God

Affirmation:

"On this day, I remain encircled in the light."

Perform this meditation in a quiet place where you will not be disturbed. Engage with the audio recording* or guide yourself through this reflection.

Meditation

I Am A Child of God Meditation

Comfortably seated and with your eyes closed, bring your focus to your heart center. Breathe deep into your core, in through your nose and out through your mouth. Allow each breath to penetrate deeper and deeper, expanding below your navel and down into the base of your body.

Slowly expand your abdomen with each inward breath. Then, expel your breath fully through your mouth while pulling your belly back in. Feel the rhythm of your heartbeat and your breath, in, out, in, out …
Relax into a steady breathing pattern now. Keep your focus upon your heart center, which is expanding and opening like a flower with each breath.

Now, locate your life force light (usually near your navel). Begin expanding that beautiful light with each breath. Note the color of your light as it continues to expand with bright clarity. Begin to send your light downward, through your tailbone, your legs, your feet—and then down through the floor and into the soil to connect with Earths' natural grounding energy. Continuing deeper, deeper, into the crystalline core of the Earth.

With your light connected to Earths' energy, they become intertwined. Now, bring them both back up through the ground, your feet, your legs, your spine and torso, all the way to your heart.

Focusing on your heart center once again, begin lifting your life light upward to your throat, your head and face, and out through your crown. Let it travel up through the clouds—up, up, into the galactic universe, where it connects with the God light.

With your light entwined with the God light, bring the two back down through the clouds, in through your crown and down through your neck to rest upon your heart. Relax and feel that the energetic pull of Mother Earth and the Universe are fully connected to your personal life force. You are aligned with, connected to, and balanced between these two polarities.

With the three energies flowing harmoniously—Earth, you, and God—continue to expand the light around your body until it totally surrounds your back, your arms, your feet, your head and every part of your body. Feel this bubble of light encompass you, shield you, hold you gently and lovingly. This is your safety bubble. Now, allow the outer barrier of your safety bubble to solidify into a tempered shell. This shell repels all that does not serve you. It absorbs only light and reflects the dark. When this barrier is in place, only pure love and light can penetrate. All negativity is repelled. You are safe in this space.

Knowing that you are continuously encased in this safety bubble of love, begin to bring your awareness back into your body. Take another deep breath in and out, visualizing your bubble of light that will travel with you always.

Worksheet

Where is your life force light located?

What color/colors do you associate with your light?

Journal your experience of connecting deep within the core of Mother Earth…

_____

_____

_____

_____

_____

Journal your experience connecting with the God Light/Universe…

_____

_____

_____

_____

_____

How did you feel within your safety bubble? What feelings/emotions did you experience? What colors? What thoughts?

_____

_____

_____

_____

_____

Your safety bubble travels with you always. Practice this exercise regularly to assist with sensing its presence.

ADDITIONAL NOTES

DAY SIX

Morning Prayer

Affirmation:

"On this day, I am grateful for my blessings."

As you wake, give thanks and gratitude for all that you have and all that you will receive throughout the day. Ask for all that lies within each encounter, conversation and feeling to be revealed to you, so that you may open to the blessing that awaits within it.

As you continue through your day, take notice of how your body moves and how your breath flows. Find comfort in all that you have, be it small or large, new or old.

When sharing time with family and friends, look deeply into your relationships and find the value, purpose and love that bring you together with each person.

At your workplace, take pride in your contribution. Find your value and be thankful for the abundance your work provides.

With each movement throughout your day and in each space that you occupy, feel the connection, look for the meaning, and fill every moment with love. Whether you are at the grocery store, having lunch, at the gym, at work, at school or simply enjoying quiet time on a park bench beside a stranger, shine your light.
Being in the moment, sharing in the joy that lies within every moment: this is where you will find your blessings. By sharing with an open heart, you receive. By showing up with your light of love, you leave an imprint of love with everyone.

Worksheet

MAKE A LIST OF YOUR GRATITUDES

What did you note about your relationships with family and friends?

At Work/School?

In which encounters did you show up (stay present in the moment) and which did you find yourself detached (letting your mind wander away)?

Whose heart did you touch today?

What blessings did you receive?

DAY SEVEN

Lessons in Life

Affirmation:

"On this day, I honor my life choices."

You have a past full of good and bad choices. These choices are how you have grown into the truth of who are in this moment. Each choice and each experience contribute to the whole.

You come to this life to learn and to grow your soul. If you came here knowing all the answers, how could you ever learn anything? How can a soul grow that is full of knowledge already?

You are not the All-Knowing. To walk in the light, you must walk in the dark. To know true love, you must experience hate. Otherwise, how can you recognize the difference?

Embrace your life path, learn from your lessons. There are blessings within the good and the bad. There is no shame in your past; by honoring your past, you are honoring yourself.

The ego self likes you to think that you are not worthy. It likes to drag you through the mud of every unwise choice made. As long as the ego keeps thinking about the past or stressing about the future, there is no room for Now.

Now is where life is. It is where the true self lives.

You are worthy. You are enough. You are perfect and simultaneously you are evolving into the brilliant soul you aspire to be. Being true to yourself is an attribute.

So, turn your lessons into blessings. Combine them with your true self and know that, in this very moment, in the presence of All That Is, you are perfect and you are creating yourself in every breath.

Worksheet

Write down a list of all of your blessings, big and small.

Then, write down all that you feel to be negative in your life.

Opposite of each negative, write a statement confirming any positive growth that came from those experiences–even if you simply write, "I learned to never do that again!"

LIST OF BLESSINGS BIG AND SMALL

Write a few words describing things which you feel have had a negative impact on your life. Next to each, write a complete statement describing any positives that came from this experience.

EXPERIENCE THAT HAD A NEGATIVE
IMPACT ON MY LIFE

POSITIVES THAT RESULTED FROM
NEGATIVE EXPERIENCE

ADDITIONAL NOTES

DAY EIGHT
My Physical Self

Affirmation:

"On this day, I embrace my physical self and vow to honor, care for, and delight in all that I am."

Who is this person I call "me"? Is this the body I'm supposed to inhabit?

Yes, it definitely is.

Before you incarnate, you chose your life's lessons, the strategies you will attempt, the actors that will be cast in the play called "my life", and who you will be in the starring role. You undertake this process with guidance from your angels, guides and spiritual council, and according to the contracts you have made with others.

One aspect of your choice is the body you will inhabit. You chose the body that will best serve and challenge you to learn the lessons you have selected in this lifetime. The shape, size, color, physical challenges and other attributes are those which will best serve the overall good for achievement.

The majority of people, when they hear this, say, "What? No way. This is not the body I want to have!" But in actuality, it is. It was specifically chosen by you to align with your soul lessons and be a home for the mind you have selected to complete the trio.

Knowing this to be true does not mean you have to like it. However, it does make it easier to accept and honor the choice you have made and learn how it fits into your life lesson.

Perhaps the physical body you chose is unhealthy, too big or too little, too tall or too small. Maybe your body is fighting itself nonstop, trying to improve. Maybe your body developed an illness even after you did all the "right" things. It is all part of the lesson.

Life is a giant puzzle meant to be assembled one piece at a time. At this very moment, reading this, you are trying to match up another piece of your puzzle. So, give yourself a break. No judgement. No criticism. No negative self-talk. Back up, connect the dots and find clarity in your reasons for choosing the body that you have. Redirect your thoughts in a positive direction so you can begin to understand and accept the reality you have created.

If you are truly unhappy with your current state, what can you do to reverse the situation? The work you undertake to heal your body may also be part of your lesson.

No matter your position, find peace with your physical self. Investigate your body; it is intricate in ways we still do not understand. Use it wisely, honor it—and, most of all, love it just as it is, for it is perfectly perfect.

Worksheet

Make of list of how your body choice has assisted you, and another of how it has challenged you.

Meditate on each list to learn your reasons for selection. Remember, it may be an emotional lesson, a joint lesson with others, or simply a learned behavior that you have adopted. It may take time to find the underlying facts—but remember, finding the answers to your body choice is the first step to embracing your truth.

ATTRIBUTE

UNDERLYING FACTS

ATTRIBUTE

UNDERLYING FACTS

ATTRIBUTE

UNDERLYING FACTS

CHALLENGE

UNDERLYING FACTS

CHALLENGE

UNDERLYING FACTS

CHALLENGE

UNDERLYING FACTS

ADDITIONAL NOTES

DAY NINE

Gift of My Family

Affirmation:

"On this day, I embrace my family and our lessons in love."

Some of us have close living families. Some of us have close arguing families. Some have family we do not even speak to. There are family members who annoy you, try to control you, and stir the family pot—and others that you cannot imagine living without.

There is variety in every family. The funny thing is, no matter the makeup of your family, you chose them, just as you chose your body and your mind.

Prior to birth, you agree (contract) with one another individually and as a group. You contracted with your family members and chose your parents to assist you with the lessons you came here to learn. Once you have passed back to the other side of the veil, your eyes open, and you are able to recognize the reasons for your challenges and find the value and benefits you received from the time spent in "Earth School" with the lessons you chose. The people and family that appear to challenge you the most are likely the ones you will thank the most on the other side. Why? They offer the greatest opportunity for growth—and growth is the biggest reason you are here.

Have you noticed the patterns within families? Patterns of many kinds exist. These patterns are established in the lineage. You can accept them, keep them, and pass them on to your offspring—or you can identify unwanted patterns and take action to break the chain. When we break the pattern, we can heal for ourselves, our children, our parents and on up and down the line for several generations in either direction. Yes, even our relatives who have passed over get the benefit of our growth—and the great thing is, it is reciprocated. If someone in your lineage heals, you get the benefit. You have upleveled, so you will vibrate on a new frequency. Whether we know it or not, we are all working for the greater good.

There are many patterns that you may choose to continue or break: family morals, acceptable standards for education and health, standards of living, alcoholism, physical or mental abuse, the partners you choose. No matter what current patterns your family is living out, no matter what role you play in others' lives, there are always lessons to be learned and opportunities for growth. The contracts between you and each player in your life are made out of love, even if, in this physical world, it is an unloving relationship.

Some chose families that are kind and loving, with little to no drama, and some chose the opposite. One choice is not better than another. The calm family has lessons embedded in their linage also. Either way, your work is to choose to view your family as gifts, no matter what they have done to you. Once you see their value and acknowledge the reasons for your contracts, you can better address and plan for change where needed.

The result? A happier, healthier, more joyful self.

Worksheet

Write out any patterns you observe within your family tree. Look at individual (one-on-one) relationship patterns, then broaden the view to locate similar patterns within your family group. Avoid dramas, the blame game and the whys—stick to the general truth.

Opposite of each identified pattern, write what the experience has taught you. Then, make a plan for change and act on it, starting right now. Once you know the truth in your core self, you can begin to live and reflect the change in your life without effort. Those around you will notice and feel the change. Some may not like it —remember, this is your experience and it is all part of the contract.

This is an ever-evolving path. Your happiness and growth are all you have to gain!

Note: You will likely add to this list as you interact with your family over the days and weeks to come. If you are uncovering a lot of information about your family contracts, you can even start a separate notebook and keep this work going for as long as needed.

FAMILY PATTERN

LESSON LEARNED

PLAN FOR CHANGE

BENEFITS I WILL RECEIVE

FAMILY PATTERN

LESSON LEARNED

PLAN FOR CHANGE

BENEFITS I WILL RECEIVE

FAMILY PATTERN

LESSON LEARNED

PLAN FOR CHANGE

BENEFITS I WILL RECEIVE

FAMILY PATTERN

LESSON LEARNED

PLAN FOR CHANGE

BENEFITS I WILL RECEIVE

DAY TEN

This Little Light of Mine

Affirmation:

"On this day, I shine my light of peace."

You have a life light. It is in the core area of your body, usually near the belly button. This is also where your spirit body is connected to your physical body.

To find your life light, sit calmly in an area with no disturbances. Close your eyes. Look within yourself using your minds' eye. Scan each area of your body slowly. Within your core, you will find your life light.

Now, observe. Where exactly is your light located? Is it bright or dim? Small or large? What color or colors does it reflect?

Continue expanding your light to completely surround your physical body. As you examine your light, cleanse away any cloudy or gray areas by surrounding them with love and asking for them to be healed. You can ask for assistance from your higher self, guides or lightworkers, angels, archangels or the God you choose on your path of trust and healing.

How your life light shines will depend on you. You can decide to nurture and grow it. You can choose to ignore it. You can choose to feed it occasionally. You even get to choose what you use it for.

(If you are in this program, it is safe to say that your life light is of importance to you.)

Focusing on your internal divine light is a great way to get familiar with and grow your energy and power. During every quiet time and meditation, take time to locate your light. Notice the size, shape and color. What emotions are attached in this moment? Practice expanding your light with each inhale and releasing any fears or emotions that are not serving you well with your exhale.

Once you become more openly connected you may feel the difference between the energies inside your body. (Once you have cleared out unwanted energies–like those cloudy, gray areas–always be sure to replace them with pure light; you do not want to leave a void in your energy field.)

By nurturing your life light, it is cleansed and can reflect more brightly within and around you. Your light shows up wherever you do and the reflection causes a ripple effect on everyone and every situation you are a part of. When you leave your imprint, it is a positive one. Sometimes others do not even know why you leave them feeling joyful by passing by. Your light is that powerful.

Worksheet

Sit quietly. Close your eyes and bring your awareness to your spirit self. Using your minds' eye, look within your core to locate your life light. With each inhale, expand your light, and with each exhale, release any fears or emotions that are not serving you well. Continue to expand your light to completely encircle your physical body.

Locate any cloudy or gray areas, send healing intention to the space and replace the old energy with pure white light.

What did you notice about your light?

SIZE

COLOR/COLORS

INTENSITY

SHAPE

Did you find any areas in need of clearing?

What process did you use to clear the energies away?

_____

_____

_____

_____

_____

Note any emotion attached and how you can keep these unwanted energies away moving forward.

_____

_____

_____

_____

_____

What positive feelings/emotions did you find during your experience?

_____

_____

_____

_____

_____

Add this practice to your daily routine. Soon you will find yourself feeling much lighter, happier and balanced.

ADDITIONAL NOTES

DAY ELEVEN

Peace and Love

Affirmation:

"On this day, I will hold only love in my heart. I feel peace settle in my soul."

Where do you find love? It is all around you! At times, it can be very hard to see. It is intertwined in every thought, action and vision you have.

Learning to see love within yourself is the first step to finding love. Once you find love within yourself, you begin to expand the love around you. You begin to breathe the light of love into your actions, your thoughts and your conversations. This expansion creates peace within and around your existence.

By infusing love into your life, you are naturally uplifted to a higher vibration. This higher vibration squeezes out and replaces any lower vibrations that no longer belong in the life you are creating.

Yes, it does often seem that life hits you right between the eyes and you have no choice but to deal with it. How you react to getting hit between the eyes is a choice though. Do you knee-jerk and snap back, or take the responsibility of fixing whatever is out of whack? Do you blame others, circumstances, or yourself—or do you evaluate the cause, determine which part of the event is truly yours to own and then plan your participation from there?

By owning up to your part in a difficult situation (without taking the blame for others) you allow yourself time to breathe in the truths that are embedded within. You can also detach much easier from your initial, dramatic reactions when you pause, shine the light of truth, accept what has happened and plan to proceed only in the areas of your lessons, letting others own their parts.

You are not the Keeper of All. You are not responsible for taking over others' lessons, only your own. You are here to love and support, not control and contribute to those lower energies. By evaluating your participation and interaction with others and using the "pause and plan" approach, you raise the vibration around yourself, limit your exposure to drama and attract peace into your life.

Be proactive in your own life, knowing that opportunities to grow and love are everywhere. Allow yourself to detach from drama without guilt. Know that, as you begin detaching, you are creating the peaceful life you deserve and are meant to live.

Worksheet

List the internal and external dramas occurring in your life right now.

Below each, note how you are responding? (If you have not addressed them yet, write about how you intend to respond.)

Now, create the higher-vibration reaction that will better serve you, and do it.

_____

_____

_____

_____

_____

_____

_____

_____

_____

_____

_____

Next, prepare for the next bit of drama that comes your way by writing out your own "Pause and Plan" strategy.

ADDITIONAL NOTES

DAY TWELVE

I Am Human

Affirmation:

"On this day, I focus my energy and thoughts on joy, and embrace my human self."

Today, evaluate the highlights and lowlights of your life choices.

Make a list of the choices that bring you joy and the duration of that joy for each choice. Do the same with the choices that have been less than positive and note the duration of the impact.

Once you are complete, evaluate. Is one list longer than the other? Did your emotions well up as you were writing? Happy, sad, pleased, remorseful … how did it feel when you placed a time frame on each? Do you tend to hang on to one emotion above others? Is there a pattern? For example, do your highlights have a lifetime guarantee or are they short returns on your investment? How about the lowlights? (No judging here. Just evaluating.)

Now, what will you do to make the highlights last longer and carry a greater joy contribution in your life? What will you do to stop the lowlight energies that have a lifetime limit written beside them?

There is an answer. There is a way to stop. It is a choice that has to be made by you. Only you can decide when enough is enough. Only you can decide when you are going to make choices aligned with your true, authentic self and the outcome you want to enjoy.

So, what if you have made choices that you have labeled as "wrong"? There are no wrong choices. There are only choices made with the information that you had at the moment of your decision. No pointing the finger at yourself here. Instead, let go of the past. There is absolutely nothing you can do to change it so why torture yourself? Mistakes are okay, and even expected. You will probably make more of them—here is the secret: that's life! That is what living in this earthly existence is all about. How you deal with your choices, how you use them to grow and how you let them go when they are done is what contributes to your enriched, truthful Now.

Yesterday is over. Breathe into the Now and embrace the moment you have before you. If you are worrying about your yesterday, you are wasting your Now. Why allow yesterdays' events to steal your joy?

Continue to grow your list of life experiences. Remember to place your focus on expanding the highs of life, diminishing the lows. The less energy and focus you allow the lows, the sooner they will be behind you for good. The more you focus your energy on the highs, the more they will show up in your life. It is the Law of Attraction at work.

Worksheet

HIGHS

DURATION

LOWS

DURATION

DAY THIRTEEN

Bathing My Colors

Affirmation:

"On this day, my thoughts remain in love. I shower myself in pure light, bathing in abundance."

"Bathing my colors" is one of the four steps to living a joyful life that were laid upon my heart many years ago. The term "colors" relates to the etheric body, which is a reflection of the physical body, with the physical being the dense, three-dimensional form and the etheric being the fluid, energetic body.

The spirit body holds the many imprints of our existence. The health of the spirit body is as important as the health of the physical and mental bodies. Keeping each healthy and aligned brings balance—meaning that you are better equipped to focus on the true meaning of existence and on your mission and contribution.

The spirit body is every bit as intricate as the physical body. It is made up of many emotions, events and thought forms. These can be positive or negative. Negativity within the etheric body shows up as dense, gray, blurry energy and even physical pain. Positivity in the etheric body shows up as bright, clear, healthy light.

Various colors appear in the different areas of the etheric body. Some, such as the chakras, are steady colors, meaning they are the same color consistently. Some change based on your experiences and what is happening around you.

"Bathing my colors" means clearing away the debris that does not serve you, in order to create space for love to enter and replace the negative energies. Joyful experiences cleanse the energy body. Wash away old patterns one layer at a time and replace them with pure, love-infused light from above. You can do this today (and every day) using the exercise from Day 10—This Little Light of Mine.

This cleansing is a process. A dedication to self. Every aspect of life contributes to your spiritual health, so address them one at a time. Peel them away, a layer at a time. Gift yourself with the time, energy and focus to cleanse your life. You are worth it. This is your experience—so make it a joyful one. (By working through this program, you are honoring yourself already!)

Worksheet

Make a list of people, places, and things that bring you joy.
Begin to incorporate them into your schedule more often.
Make a date with yourself by penciling them in on your calendar.

JOY   DATE

JOY   DATE

_____   _____

_____   _____

_____   _____

_____   _____

_____   _____

_____   _____

_____   _____

_____   _____

_____   _____

_____   _____

_____   _____

_____   _____

ADDITIONAL NOTES

94

DAY FOURTEEN

Cleanse the Past

Affirmation:

"On this day, I am free in my Now."

This is a continuation of yesterdays' "Bathing My Colors".

Yesterday, you saw yourself as the beautiful, flowing, ever-evolving array of the colors of your true self. Today, you will release yourself from your past.

Using your worksheet, make a list of the events, circumstances and people (yourself included) that have muddied your thoughts and weighed on your heart. Write out an intention as you release each. For example: "I recognize you, (fill in the name), as a participant in this situation. I release all attachment of emotion, surround you in love and free myself completely."

In a quiet, calm, place, sit comfortably, close your eyes and begin to breathe in pure light frequencies. Feel yourself infused with light energy. Let it expand throughout your body, surrounding you completely. As you exhale, release all tensions, thoughts and responsibilities.

Picture yourself in nature. There is a large waterfall in front of you, surrounded by a rainbow of colors. One by one, place each person or event that you want to release under the waterfall. Recognize. Cleanse. Release. Free yourself. Take all the time needed for each one, honoring the emotions that arise. Be certain that you have cleared all energies and emotions associated with the person or event before moving on to the next.

Move through the list. Once you have completed the list, hold the high intention of releasing all bindings to these people and events, now that they have been cleansed completely. Feel your vibration rise as you heal. Now, burn the list you wrote.

This is an ongoing practice. You may have new things appear in your daily experiences that need to be cleansed. Old wounds may also arise that do not serve you in your current elevated space. Repeat this cleansing as often as needed to release what you no longer need. Feel the truth of who you really are revealed as you cleanse away the layers of the past.

Worksheet

Make a list of the events, circumstances and people (yourself included) that have muddied your thoughts and weighed on your heart.

Write out an intention to use as you release each. For example: "I recognize (fill in the name) as a participant in this situation. I release all attachment of emotion, surround you in love and free myself completely."

When you are done and have performed the visualization, tear out this page and burn it. (Or make your list in a separate notebook.)

NAME / EVENT

RELEASE INTENTION

NAME / EVENT

RELEASE INTENTION

_____

_____

_____

NAME/ EVENT

_____

_____

_____

RELEASE INTENTION

_____

_____

_____

NAME/ EVENT

_____

_____

_____

RELEASE INTENTION

_____

_____

_____

ADDITIONAL NOTES

DAY FIFTEEN

Joy

Affirmation:

"On this day, I will imprint joy, staying present in the moment."

Todays' heart-opening experience is a continuation of the past two days' exercises. First, you bathed your colors; then, you cleansed the past. Now, you will spread the joy.

I trust that you have been successful with purging the past and are beginning to see your true, authentic self as the powerful, bright light that you are. If you are not there yet, please take the time to continue your cleansing process, as each repetition will bring you closer to your core self.

Each day—in fact, each moment—offers an opportunity to spread joy. This is true whether you are at work or school, with family or friends, or just sitting alone. Joy is a state of mind and a state of heart. It radiates around you and touches everyone in every situation. When you are in joy, you leave an imprint.

It is up to you to decide what imprint you want to leave. If you are not sure, consider adopting a positive motto such as, "I want everyone I encounter to feel better about themselves when we part ways".

By spreading joy and sharing the love of your open heart, you are leaving a positive imprint. The action you take could be a small compliment, a brief smile or wave or an unexpected act of kindness—even if the recipient does not know you are the source of their brighter day, you will feel the return of the energy of joy you have put out. Again, this is the Law of Attraction: what you put out is what you receive. Wouldn't you love to receive joy and positive, uplifting waves of energy all day, every day? Choose joy in your life!

Being present in the "Now" moment of each breath is where you will find ample opportunity to spread joy. It is when you are tied up in the past or the "things to do" lists that you miss opportunities to find and spread joy. Letting these opportunities pass by leaves a void or a hole in the energy space. What will fill that void? Worry, stress or past memories. Why have those things when you could fill your moments with love, joy and fellowship?

Leave your imprint of joy. Remember, it all comes back to you.

Worksheet

Create your own special motto as a reminder of the imprint you want to leave on people, on situations and within your own heart.

For example: "I want everyone I encounter to feel better about themselves when we part ways."

MY MOTTO

_____

_____

_____

_____

_____

_____

DAY SIXTEEN

God's Promise

Affirmation:

"On this day, I practice my faith surrounded in love and peace."

Living life based on promises takes a lot of faith. Today, you will practice faith.

By aligning with God's promise of love, you find peace in your heart. To enjoy this state of bliss requires faith. Faith is invisible and difficult at times to maintain. As you grow closer to your truth, your faith will naturally evolve.

Faith grows when you place yourself in line with the path of truth, practice sharing love, balance yourself through difficult times and remain steadfast through doubt. Faith grows when you pick yourself up after a fall and keep your focus on the knowledge of your personal connection to God, Creator, Source and Higher Power. As life unveils itself, you will find direction, reason and a deliverance of faith.

Some have faith already and will continue to grow in faith as truth seekers. Some are looking for faith and some believe they cannot have it. None is better, none is less. In the end, we all seek the same source. We may be on different paths, yet we are going the same direction. One is not a quicker or a holier route. God loves us equally as we are.

The promise of peace and the promise of love lie in and around you. With diligence, you will open your eyes and heart to receive. The only block to faith is what is created in the mind. Realize that you are worthy and deserving of peace and love. Seek what you desire. Open yourself to receive and watch as you manifest these promises. Then, take these promises and own them in your heart.

Print and carry the worksheet as a tool for today's practice. There are four columns labeled Experience, Love, Peace, Faith. After each conversation, task, event, or thought, jot down a relatable word to prompt your memory of the experience. Make a checkmark beside each after you reflect to determine if you found the gift of love and/or peace in the experience. (If not, reexamine, because a gift lies within every experience.) Then ask yourself if you practiced faith in this interaction; use a plus or minus sign in this column to denote your level of faith.

At the end of the day, review your notes without judgement and without reliving the events in depth. Notice any patterns.

As you continue to grow your faith, your columns will begin to fill up. Try this same practice again after a few weeks. Notice the changes and see how you have grown your faith.

Worksheet

EXPERIENCE	LOVE	PEACE	FAITH +/-

DAY SEVENTEEN

Focusing My View

Affirmation:

"On this day, I begin my self-discovery, aligning with my authentic self."

At birth, you arrived in a pure state with full and complete trust that your needs would be met and that someone would be there continuously. You had no doubt that all is good and being helpless is of no concern. All you had to do is yell and someone would answer. As a baby, you viewed the world as all-available and fully capable of providing exactly what you needed and desired. There was no judgement, only trust.

As you grow and move through life, you quickly conform. There is so much drama, so much fear, so many opinions on how to behave, what to think, what to wear, who to be. But what about who you are? Where did that go?

Think about it: if you were to wipe away the thoughts instilled in you by your peers, parents, teachers and the ego, what would be left? Your pure self, as open and innocent as you were at birth–and a beautiful opportunity to recreate yourself.

It would be nice to part ways with the brainwashing that may have, up until now, kept you from knowing who you are truly meant to be. You cannot blame others. They did the best they could, as you have, and they acted according to the contracts you made with them. The madness does not have to continue once you know it for what it is. You can reset and align with your truths.

That is what you are going to do today.

Start a self-discovery journal. (Do not worry–you will have plenty to fill it in the days and weeks to come.) In it, write something simple, like "Clothing Style". Ask yourself, "Does my style reflect me, or those around me? Do I adhere to what is expected or do I place a hint of my own flare even when I need to conform to dress codes for work, exercise or social gatherings?"

Other topics for consideration are your political and religious views and practices, how you relate to and converse with others and how you decorate your home. Examine the car you drive, the foods you eat and the words you say. Are they original or are you repeating a learned phrase or behavior?

Incorporate this self-evaluation into your daily life to reveal what is you and what is learned behavior. If you like what you are doing, keep at it; if not, adjust the pattern and rewrite it to reflect your beliefs.

The importance of this exercise is to discover your inner self and live authentically. Even if you change an aspect of yourself today to align with your identity, it will likely change again. You are an ever-evolving soul. You will be focused when you are coming from an authentic place.

Worksheet

PERSONAL ASPECT OF SELF

Authentic or Learned Behavior

○ AUTHENTIC   ○ LEARNED BEHAVIOR

If it is a Learned Behavior, where/who did I learn this from?

_____

_____

_____

_____

What is my true belief?

_____

_____

_____

_____

How am I willing to recreate this behavior to reflect my authentic self?

_____

_____

_____

_____

PERSONAL ASPECT OF SELF

Authentic or Learned Behavior

◯ AUTHENTIC   ◯ LEARNED BEHAVIOR

If it is a Learned Behavior, where/who did I learn this from?

_____

_____

_____

_____

What is my true belief?

_____

_____

_____

_____

How am I willing to recreate this behavior to reflect my authentic self?

_____

_____

_____

_____

PERSONAL ASPECT OF SELF

Authentic or Learned Behavior

◯ AUTHENTIC   ◯ LEARNED BEHAVIOR

If it is a Learned Behavior, where/who did I learn this from?

What is my true belief?

How am I willing to recreate this behavior to reflect my authentic self?

DAY EIGHTEEN

Clarity

Affirmation:

"On this day, my heart is open to receiving."

The first moments of awakening in the morning (when an alarm is not rattling in your ear) are when you are most open to the other side of the veil. This is the most opportune time for your loved ones, guides and angels to connect with you through dreams, songs, visions, smells and emotions. If you listen, you may even hear someone say your name.

Your guides want to converse with you and use every opportunity to communicate. Throughout the day, you may notice a repeat of a particular word or phrase, a song or a name. These may be signs that your guides are trying to get your attention. All you have to do is notice the signs and put the pieces together.

This sounds easy; however, it is a challenge at first. Living in the world, remembering all that needs to be done and noticing your surroundings all at the same time takes practice. It is a learned skill. As with all things, when you practice noticing signs, it will become second nature for you.

Today, practice listening with intent and seeing with expanded vision, taking in all that surrounds you. At the end of the day, pull the pieces together and look for consistencies. It may take a few days of observation to put the clues together.

Meanwhile, take advantage of the twilight time you are experiencing right now. Start a dream journal. (This is just a notebook that you keep by your bed.) When you wake up naturally, even if it is in the middle of the night, relax into your emotions and thoughts. Recall any impressions that you may have felt as you began waking up. Notice any smells associated with the memory. Maybe you feel an emotion that reminds you of your past, or you suddenly have clarity around a project or adventure you have been pondering.

Take your time and be in the moment, allowing all of your senses to remain heightened.

Once you feel complete in the message, journal your thoughts. Also, take note of the time when you open your eyes to look at the clock. A message may be in the numbers or today's date.

Take thorough notes. Some may not make sense when you write them. In review, you may find connections. Either way, trust that you are being guided and loved in every way.

Worksheet

USE THE SPACE PROVIDED ON THE

FOLLOWING PAGES TO RECORD YOUR

DREAMS AT ANY POINT DURING YOUR

SOUL EXPANSION JOURNEY.

MY DREAM JOURNAL

DATE _____   TIME _____

DREAM/EXPERIENCE

_____

_____

_____

_____

_____

_____

_____

_____

_____

_____

_____

_____

_____

EMOTIONS AND THOUGHTS SURROUNDING MY DREAM/EXPERIENCE

MEMORY STIMULATED/SMELLS ASSOCIATED/IDEAS/CONFIRMATIONS

MY DREAM JOURNAL

DATE _____   TIME _____

DREAM/EXPERIENCE

_____

_____

_____

_____

_____

_____

_____

_____

_____

_____

_____

_____

EMOTIONS AND THOUGHTS SURROUNDING MY DREAM/EXPERIENCE

MEMORY STIMULATED/SMELLS ASSOCIATED/IDEAS/CONFIRMATIONS

MY DREAM JOURNAL

DATE _____   TIME _____

DREAM/EXPERIENCE

_____

_____

_____

_____

_____

_____

_____

_____

_____

_____

_____

_____

_____

_____

EMOTIONS AND THOUGHTS SURROUNDING MY DREAM/EXPERIENCE

MEMORY STIMULATED/SMELLS ASSOCIATED/IDEAS/CONFIRMATIONS

MY DREAM JOURNAL

DATE _____   TIME _____

DREAM/EXPERIENCE

_____

_____

_____

_____

_____

_____

_____

_____

_____

_____

_____

_____

_____

EMOTIONS AND THOUGHTS SURROUNDING MY DREAM/EXPERIENCE

MEMORY STIMULATED/SMELLS ASSOCIATED/IDEAS/CONFIRMATIONS

DAY NINETEEN

One with God

Affirmation:

"On this day, I am one with God."

When a soul transitions from this world, what happens?

We are all dying, aren't we? We are born, we spend our time growing and learning until the moment comes when we have completed the mission, then we close this chapter and start a new one.

There is no need for fear of death. It is all familiar territory. You have been there before. That is where you originated.

Before arriving in this world, you are a part of another world. When you leave this world, you are simply returning to where you came from. It is a different reality where you are able to see more clearly and where you are finally free of the dense, heavy feeling of the physical body. Upon arrival, you get to look back and review this lifetime of experiences with eyes wide open. During this review, you feel on a deeply emotional level. You experience the ripple effect of your words and actions over your lifetime, both positive and negative. During the visit on earth, a soul aspires to become one with God, one with the higher consciousness. The truth is, you were never separated. In birth a soul chooses to forget; the life endeavor is truth-seeking. The goal at the end is to have grown closer to God–to have expanded in knowledge, and to have a clear vision of truth in self, truth in God and truth in our connection.

To assist in connecting the dots between birth and death, mark a date on your calendar exactly six months from today. Now, write a letter addressed to yourself. In this letter, address any and all concerns or fears you may have as related to your transition from this world into the next. Also, list your hopes, visions and any comforts and beliefs you have associated with your departure. Be specific and be truthful. Let the letter flow. Sign and date your letter, seal it in an envelope, mark it with the date you chose six months from now and put it in a safe place. (Leave yourself a hint on your calendar as to where you put it.) Then, put the letter out of your thoughts.

In six months, write another letter, using the same outline, to be opened in six more months. Before you seal the new letter away, open the first letter. Read it closely and note the changes surrounding all three categories. As you shift your consciousness over time, you will shift your fears about death and what comes after as well. Moving away from fear-based thoughts brings you closer to the truth: You are never separate from God.

Worksheet

Dear Self,

These are my current concerns and fears as related to transitioning . . .

My comforts and beliefs are . . .

I hope and visualize my afterlife as . . .

Love,

(SELF)

(DATE)

DAY TWENTY

Into the Light

Affirmation:

"On this day, I remain in the light. I am the light."

Walking in the light feels like gliding instead of walking. You feel light on your feet and light in your heart. Walking in the light is like spending your day floating around, tossing happy little sprinkles everywhere you go. As with anything worthy of attention, practice and focus are essential. Then it will become a natural part of your daily existence.

Visualize a light streaming from above, landing in and around your whole body—pouring in through your head, then bursting into a complete bubble, encasing you safely.

Keep your light bright and shining around you everywhere you go. Feel it as it reflects back on you. You will exuberate confidence while encased in your safety bubble.

You have worked with your protective bubble of light already. This time, play with the energy and allow it to become more familiar.

Get your happy bubble of light in place now.

Find a quiet place to sit comfortably for this visualization session. Engage with the audio recording* or guide yourself through this reflection.

*You can download an audio version of this guided meditation at https://thesoulsharmony.com/40-Day-Soul-Expansion-Download/

Meditation

Into the Light Meditation

Release all of your worries and concerns. Extend your awareness up beyond your body, beyond the room, the sky. Continue up into the galactic and beyond, accessing the bliss of all oneness. See the spark of the God-light as it approaches you. Now, it connects with you and travels back down with you through the universe, the clouds, the room—back in through your crown, intertwined with your heart.

Bring your awareness to your breath. Notice how the light begins to grow with each inhalation.

Now, with each breath, expand your light slowly, covering your arms and legs, your back, your head Let the pure light of God fully surround you now.

Notice the outer edges of your bubble of light. It has a shell of mirrors all around it. This mirror encasement totally absorbs all light and good while deflecting any dark energies away from you.

You are safe as you rest in the light.

Practice bringing the light back in closer, letting the bubble get smaller. Notice how you feel. Now with your breath, expand your light once again. Notice how you feel in this expanded state. You are light hearted, joyful, radiant and safe in your bubble of light.

Leaving your bubble in place, begin to bring your awareness back into your body, waking the body up, moving your fingers and toes, stretching your arms. With eyes open, you are ready to go about your day, knowing your bubble of light travels with you always.

Worksheet

Practice the expansion and contraction of your bubble of light to become more familiar with the energy. As you become familiar, you will start to "know" and "feel" the energy around you.

Journal your experience of being surrounded by your safety bubble.

HOW DOES IT FEEL? (soft/smooth/comforting/strong/secure)

HOW DO YOU FEEL?

DO YOU SENSE AN EMOTION?

IS THERE COLOR/COLORS IN YOUR BUBBLE?

DO YOU SENSE THE TINY MIRRORS ABSORBING AND REFLECTING?

Journal you experience of your light in its smaller state within you.

HOW DOES IT FEEL? soft/smooth/comforting/strong/secure

HOW DO YOU FEEL?

WHAT DOES THIS SMALLER ENERGY FEEL LIKE?

WHAT IS THE DIFFERENCE BETWEEN THE EXPANDED VS SMALLER LIGHT?

Hold the vision and energy you have identified as your expanded safety bubble. Practice remaining in this bubble always. It will become second nature.

DAY TWENTY-ONE

Release

Affirmation:

"On this day, I am free."

Releasing yourself from the bondage of the past is a big, big step. The work you have done thus far may have felt like an emotional rollercoaster filled with highs and lows, love and fear, as you connected with those parts of your life that you used to keep hidden in the closet. In the closet, they fester, linger and never heal. That is not healthy, which is why you have opened up the door and started airing it out. You have even addressed some of the ugliness and pain, sending it out the window.

It is time now to finish the job. It is time to turn on the light, bleach the floors and walls and redecorate.

What is left in your closet? Self-doubt, guilt or unforgiveness? Or, maybe there is someone you would like to ask for forgiveness. Look closely. Today you are getting it all out.

Carry today's worksheet with you and begin writing down each item as you pull it out, leaving nothing behind. Be honest about what is still in your closet. Leave nothing unexplored.

When your list is complete and your closet is empty, you may feel a bit anxious and overwhelmed. That is okay, you are going to start the release party! (Yes, it is a "party". When you are done with today's exercise, you will be ready to celebrate!)

Looking at one item at a time, apply the following to each, writing out your answers.

1. Is this truly mine to own?

2. If it is yours, write a statement, confirming your participation, being truthful with yourself.

3. List all parties involved, whether they instigated, assisted, or were hurt from this action. Do not forget yourself.

4. Now, draw a line through the names of everyone involved except those who were hurt. Who is left? Those who suffered and you.

5. Next, write a brief and meaningful apology to each person left on the list, including yourself.

Now, it is action time. As you review this list and the apologies, notice your feelings and emotions. Do you feel the need to ask for forgiveness? Whether the person is here in the physical realm or alive in spirit, this can be accomplished. No one is judging you and no one is holding your feet to the fire. Only you know the answer.

Remember, when you ask for forgiveness, you must detach from the outcome. The receiver has a choice to accept or decline.

It is necessary to ask yourself for forgiveness. This is not optional. State out loud: "I forgive myself for _____ (describe the event) and release all attachment, judgment and hurt to the light."

Once you have completed an item on your list, let it go. You can burn it, shred it, whatever brings you release. It is important to remove it completely from your space.

With your closet cleaned and your heart free, you are ready to start redecorating. Fill that space with things that bring you joy.

Worksheet

Make a separate copy of this worksheet for each closet item. (Or, create your own worksheet in a notebook.)
How do you feel?

ITEM IN YOUR CLOSET:

1. Is this truly mine to own?

2. If it is yours, write a statement confirming your participation, being truthful with yourself.

3. List all parties involved, whether they instigated, assisted, or were hurt from this action. Do not forget yourself.

4. Now, draw a line through the names of everyone involved except those who were hurt. Who is left? Those who suffered and you.

5. Next, write a brief and meaningful apology to each person left on the list, including yourself.

It is action time. Decide if you will be apologizing directly to the person or persons. If so, make a plan and give yourself an exact date that you will take care of relaying the apology. Remember, you are heard even when speaking to spirit.

Next, apologize to yourself. Looking into your own eyes in a mirror, state out loud,

"I forgive myself for ____ (describe the event) and release all attachment, judgment and hurt to the light."

After you have completed each item, burn this paper, shred it or release it in any way that removes it from your space. Then, move on to the next item on your list.

I FORGIVE MYSELF FOR:

I FORGIVE MYSELF FOR:

DAY TWENTY-TWO

Time

Affirmation:

"On this day, I live each segment of my life in joy."

Time. Is it measurable? Do you live by the clock? Does the clock control you?

It does in many ways. There is a time to go to school, a time for work, a time to prepare dinner. There is a time to wake up and a time to go to bed. Then, there are other aspects of time: time to move on, time to get with the program, time for a change.

How can you get the most out of the time you have?

It is an important question. Although the hands on the clock determine your schedules, there is still the time in between—your personal free time—and how your thoughts and attitude show up in those moments can make a big difference in how you feel.

Time is broken down into segments like work, leisure, sleep and many others. How you segment your day is up to you. Yes, earning a living is important; maintaining relationships, feeding and caring for the body, etc. are as well. However, there is no need to push so hard to fit ten hours of responsibilities into five hours of time. Instead, use your time in way that flows naturally and brings balance and satisfaction your way.

There must be balance. There must be breathing room. If not, we become stressed, exhausted mentally and physically. Worse, we begin to drop the ball (or many balls) and end up disappointed in ourselves. It is also important to be flexible with your schedule whenever possible. Deviate from the plan and ask for help when necessary.

Today, take a close look at how you segment your days, your weeks and weekends, the months, the years. Do you leave space for breathing, relaxing and "me time"? If not, it is time for a change.

Are you enjoying each segment of your day? Do you spend more time in front of the TV or your computer than you do enjoying your hobbies? Is it time to switch out your exercise program or start a new one? Find the imbalances, plan out your options and make the change.

By decluttering your time and enjoying the time you have, you will create a happier, healthier, balanced you.

Worksheet

By logging your time, you can easily look back to see where you have spent it all. You can also use time logging as a tool to help with delegation, elimination of unnecessary tasks and rearranging schedules to feel more balanced.

On a separate sheet of paper, keep track of how you fill you days for one consecutive week using the example below.

DAY 1

DATE .... DAY OF THE WEEK ....

MORNING SEGMENT:

TASK .... TIME SPENT ....

TASK .... TIME SPENT ....

AFTERNOON SEGMENT:

TASK .... TIME SPENT ....

TASK .... TIME SPENT ....

EVENING SEGMENT:

TASK .... TIME SPENT ....

TASK .... TIME SPENT ....

At the end of a week, review your time.

Do you have more responsibilities than will fit on your paper? If so, what can be delegated to someone else? How can you rearrange your time to make it more efficient? Did you fit in "me time"? Did you leave yourself room to breathe? Using what you have learned in this exercise, begin to tweak your days/weeks to fit your needs and desires for yourself.

DAY TWENTY-THREE

Soul Awakening

Affirmation:

"On this day, I vow to stand fully in my truths, living them out loud."

When you made the decision to commit to this program, you committed to your own awakening. Your transformation may be beginning or you may be well on your way. Either way, you have shown up in your life! You are committing to yourself and to honoring your spiritual being.

Soul awakening rises at various times. Some are born with a knowing that they are here for a higher purpose and some may never reach the point of awakening. Guess what? It is okay either way. As humans, we do the best we can with the information that we have.

You are on your path of awakening and today you are going to tap in to your personal GPS to uncover a bit more about your direction, your passions and your contribution to humankind and the collective consciousness.

First, center and ground yourself, connecting to your heart center and your lower core self. (You can access this space using our previous practices.) Clear your mind. Regulate your breath, bringing it deep into your core. Expand your life light, connecting to the God light.

Once you are in your connected, elevated, safe space, ask the question, "What is my purpose in this lifetime?" Journal your answer.

Then, with pencil in hand, follow with this series of questions. Write out your first thought after each question without judgment, so your head does not get involved.

1. What are my top 3 qualities?

2. What activity/interaction brings me the most joy?

3. What environments or group of people am I most comfortable around?

4. Where do I seek solace?

5. What thoughts do I have that stimulate my soul?

6. If others were to describe me, what would be their top three words?

Take a look at your answers. This is the essence of who you are when standing within your true self. Soak in these words and feel how they resonate with your soul.

Now, rewrite each of your answers as statements. For example: if you answered "Kind, openhearted, generous" to question #1, your statement would be something like, "I am a kind, generous person who shows up with an open heart."

Complete a separate statement for all six questions. These statements will become your daily affirmations. Write each of these sentences at least once a day—even more, if possible. Pay attention to the emotions attached to each statement. Feel them to be true for you.

This is a great starting place. Be aware that your daily affirmations will change as you develop. You will know when it is time to adjust or add to your affirmations. They will start to feel too "small" for you. Intuitively and naturally, your affirmations will begin to shift as you align with your true self blueprint.

Worksheet

Once you are in your connected, elevated, safe space, ask the question:

How do I serve in this lifetime?

_____

_____

_____

_____

_____

Next, begin this series of questions, taking your first of thought after each question, not letting your head get involved.

1. What are my top three qualities?

_____

2. What activity/interaction brings me the most joy? (2-3)

_____

3. What environment or group of people am I most comfortable around? (2-3)

_____

4. Where do I seek solace?

_____

_____

_____

_____

_____

_____

_____

5. What thoughts do I have that stimulate my soul? (at least 3)

_____

_____

_____

_____

_____

_____

_____

6. If others were to describe me, what would be their top three words?

_____   _____   _____

Review your answers and create statements from each.

These are your daily affirmations. Write out these statements once a day. Feel them to be true for you.

DAY TWENTY-FOUR

Discernment

Affirmation:

"On this day, I hold my space and share my energy through positive, loving channels."

Discernment is the ability to know and feel the difference between positive and negative, good and bad.

Discernment appears as the "butterfly" feeling in your heart when you feel love or joy, or as the panicked, anxious, nervous feeling you feel when faced with drama or fear. Those are easy to recognize. Other feelings are more subtle; that is why this review is prompting you to look deeper into your feelings, relationships and environments.

You are not looking from a place of judgement; you are looking from a place of knowing. It is important to know who you are safe with and where you are safe—not just physically safe, also emotionally and energetically safe.

For example, there may be someone in your world who, without their awareness, feeds on the energy of others. To attain the level of feeling, emotion or fulfillment desired, they seek outside sources. They are not able to generate it on their own. This type of personality is a "psychic vampire". You may encounter them anywhere: in your circle of friends, at work or school, within your family or in random encounters.

Sharing energy is a beautiful, uplifting feeling—when you have agreed to it. Being robbed of your energy is never good. Practice discernment to protect your energy from those who take it without asking.
Here are a few ways to practice discernment.

1. Keep yourself in your safety bubble of protection. When you are in your safety bubble, all negativity and attempts to use your energy will be reflected away from you.

2. Avoid getting sucked into someone else's drama. That is their reality, not yours. You choose what to create and accept into your own reality.

3. In every encounter—at work, in the grocery store, or at home—ask yourself the following questions: *

- Does this person trust themselves?

- Can I trust them?

- Is the conversation uplifting or drama-filled?

This content is, in part, adapted from conversations with my Life Coach, Dr. Carol McCall, PhD, MCC, Founder, of The Institute for Global Listening and Communication, LLC. You can learn more about Dr. Carol at www.listeningprofitsu.com.

- Do I find myself fully present or drifting?

- Am I fully engaged and interested?

- Is the personality before me large and captivating?

- If I disagree, am I redirected until I see things their way?

- Am I calm and relaxed, or jittery and confused?

- After I part ways with this person, am I tired and drained?

- Have I been manipulated or violated?

- Is there a sense of uncertainty of self?

- What did I gain from this encounter, and what did the other person look to gain or achieve from this encounter?

Any of the above statements, when answered from a true self point, will have emotion attached. How does that emotion feel? Does it resonate nicely or is there resistance?

Not everyone is out to steal your energy. Some love and honor you, as you do them. Practicing discernment and working with the above questions will give you valuable information about the people in your world and how you can stop the drain where it is happening.

As with all things, discernment gets easier with practice. Practice without judgment of self. Keep asking the questions, until you know instinctively when to expand your safety bubble and when it is safe for you to let your shields down.

Worksheet

Practice applying these questions to all of your interactions to begin discerning the difference between positive, loving conversations and dramatic, draining conversations. Once you become more familiar with these feelings, you will be able to quickly discern what is right for you and what people or places are not serving you well.

Apply these questions to assist with discernment.

1. Does this person trust themselves?

2. Can I trust them?

3. Is the conversation uplifting or drama-filled?

4. Do I find myself fully present or drifting?

5. Am I fully engaged and interested?

6. Is the personality before me large and captivating?

7. If I disagree, am I redirected until I see things their way?

8. Am I calm and relaxed, or jittery and confused?

9. After I part ways with this person, am I tired and drained?

10. Have I been manipulated or violated?

11. Is there a sense of uncertainty of self?

12. What did I gain from this encounter, and what did the other person look to gain or achieve from this encounter?

Any of the above statements, when answered from a true self point, will have emotion attached. How does that emotion feel? Does it resonate nicely or is there resistance?

ADDITIONAL NOTES

ADDITIONAL NOTES

DAY TWENTY-FIVE

The Power of the Unseen

Affirmation:

"On this day, I commit to my heart's desires."

The Power of the Unseen lies within.

You have control over what you say, what you do, how you react or handle yourself. You control your life choices and your morals; this is your play. How you show up and what character you portray, is totally your choice.

Kind of scary, right?

You are not only the lead actor; you are also the director of your play. You stage scenes, assign characters, change the background scenery and even write the script and the soundtrack.

As you move through your life, you change, the play takes on a new plot. Changing to the next storyline is good and normal—so how do you show up in these new scenes? Is your character evolving slowly, rapidly or not at all? Is your character learning and maturing?

Producing a great play takes lots and lots of behind-the-scenes work. This life is your play. It is your story and your reality. Leading it to unfold according to the message of your heart and the desires of your soul, will require planning.

Today, you are going to plot out your next scene using your worksheet.
Once you have put your thoughts down on paper, make a plan to start acting out this new play. The sooner the curtains open, the sooner you will begin living out your desires.

Worksheet

Ask and answer the following questions to assist with plotting out your play.

1. What are my hearts desires? (list them all)

_____

_____

_____

_____

_____

_____

_____

_____

_____

_____

_____

2. What environment or environments compliment my desires?

3. What types of characters will fulfill my hearts desires? Are they within my circle, or does it require auditions to add or replace key characters?

4. How will I support this play (i.e., income source)?

5. What tools are required to perform at my fullest capacity (education, self-help programs, support system)?

6. What message am I relaying? What is my contribution in this world?

7. How will I show up? What kind of lead character will I be?

8. What are my goal achievements in review? What is the apex of the plot?

Make an action plan from your thoughts. Review your answers periodically.

DAY TWENTY-SIX

Give and Take

Affirmation:

"On this day, my heart flows openly, elevated in love."

Today, the focus is on your heart. The heart is the middle energy center and sends love in both directions.

From the heart, love pours down to the solar plexus, where you will find your personal power; to the sacral energy center, the emotional self; and to the root, the survival center and the root of your being. These three energy centers are your guideposts in the physical realm.

The heart sends love upward also: to the throat, the expression and truth; to the third eye, the intuition or "sixth sense"; and to the crown, which is the universal connection. These three are the energy centers associated with spirituality.

With the heart open and flowing, love radiates all around. Others can feel that love.

When you spend time with someone—even if it is just a short exchange of words, a smile or a laugh—their energy can be felt. Energy radiates all around the body. It may not always be love energy; it may also be anger, sadness, giddiness or seriousness. When the mood changes, the frequency of the energy field changes also and is emitted all around. This affects those in the room or space and ripples out across the whole world.

Today, observe and play with your energy (yours and others') for a clearer understanding of the effects of your mood on others.

Beginning with yourself, check your mood. How would you describe it? As you move through your day, notice how your mood shifts depending upon where you are, what you are doing and who you are with. Notice the way the air feels around you, how others react to you. Feel the exchanges of energy and how your mood affects your enthusiasm and productivity.

Chart these feelings and exchanges each time your environment, task or internal feelings shift.

Next, bring your attention to the energy you feel coming from other people and the spaces you spend time in. (Even an empty room can hold energetic vibrations!) Do these outside energies change how you feel? Are you lifted from a solemn or bad mood by others' happiness? Dragged down from a happy mood by a negative

---

*This content is, in part, adapted from conversations with my Life Coach, Dr. Carol McCall, PhD, MCC, Founder, of The Institute for Global Listening and Communication, LLC. You can learn more about Dr. Carol at www.listeningprofitsu.com.

space? Chart these experiences on your worksheet.

At the end of the day, look for patterns, consistencies or fluctuations in how you showed up and how (and to what degree) the energies around you may have shifted your mood.

Now that you are familiar with and can recognize the effects' you have on others and how you process their energies, apply your new awareness to your daily life. Strive to keep your vibration elevated to emit positive love energy in and around yourself, to others, and out into the world.

Worksheet

This is an outline to assist with assessment of your day. Use additional notepaper to keep track of each mood shift and change of environment.

Adjective Describing My Mood

_____

_____

_____

How does my mood affect my enthusiasm and productivity?

_____

_____

_____

How do others react to my mood?

_____

_____

_____

What is my environment, and who are the people around me?

_____

_____

_____

What is their mood?

_____

_____

_____

How am I affected?

_____

_____

_____

Do I adjust to the frequencies around me? If so, to what degree?

_____

_____

_____

At the end of the day, look for patterns, consistencies or fluctuations.

Noticing the effects of the energies you emit and receive can assist with learning to maintain a higher vibration at all times.

ADDITIONAL NOTES

DAY TWENTY-SEVEN

Life's Storms

Affirmation:

"On this day, I send love and support to all in need."

Life is full of many storms. Some consist of a light drizzle, others wreak havoc as if lightning bolted right through your body.

There are times when you are faced with difficult, even heart-wrenching situations, and ask, "Why me? Why did this happen to me?" The answer is that there are various contributing factors in play. One is the pre-planning of your life that takes place prior to birth. Earth School is an opportunity to grow the soul. The other is your free-will choices and the thoughts you think every day, which create your reality.

In order to grow the soul, there must be experiences. These experiences are chosen during the planning stage and those who are a part of these experiences have agreed or contracted to participate. It is a group effort. Our free will impacts the outcome of the plan and which direction we flow.

For example, one of the most difficult experiences for anyone is when a child becomes ill and passes.

As difficult as it may seem, that little soul agreed to carry that burden for the greater good of his or her soul group. How brave. What a beautiful act of love.

Now, look at the impact of this on the child's parents, siblings, family, friends and community. Look at the empathy stimulated amongst the people at school, workplaces, medical facilities, charity organizations, even the local news. Look at the ripple effect and how many are impacted. By this one event, dozens, hundreds, maybe thousands of people are stimulated to take action. People begin speaking about their experiences, sharing their stories. Scholarships and research funds are created. Parks are built. Action is taken for the greater good.

How you react and process the emotions of life's storms is fundamental to your soul growth. Today, briefly reflect on a recent "storm" in your life—not focusing on the tragedy itself. Focus on any positives that you have witnessed as a "ripple effect" of that event. Lift up those who were affected in your prayers, sending your love and support to both sides of the veil. Remember to focus on the light side, keeping your awareness on positive outcomes only.

Worksheet

EVENT:

_____

_____

IMMEDIATE SOUL GROUP:

_____   _____

_____   _____

INTERMEDIATE SUB GROUPS:

_____   _____

_____   _____

EXTENDED SUB GROUPS:

_____   _____

_____   _____

Note the positive impacts you have noticed. These can be personal, or more general. Look closely and list as many as you can.

_____

_____

_____

_____

YOU (What group do you fall in? Briefly list any actions prompted in you):

SOUL GROUP

MY ACTIONS

Take time to send love and healing thoughts to all.

DAY TWENTY-EIGHT

Beyond the Veil

Affirmation:

"On this day, I send love to the other side of the veil."

When a soul transitions from this life, those left behind mourn for their loss. Meanwhile, the one who has transitioned is bursting with excitement. They are reunited with those they love—only this time, it is with eyes wide open and without the heaviness of the physical body. Communication in the realms beyond the veil is telepathic. Transportation is as quick as a thought. Colors are more vibrant. Opportunities are limitless.

When a soul is ready to move on and leave the physical body behind, a welcoming party gathers. It is truly a party. The cherubs blow their trumpets announcing the arrival. Angels sing. Sweet, soft music plays. It is a big event.

The soul is eternal. The human body is borrowed as part of the lesson plan. The soul does not die when the physical body is shed; instead, the soul continues to live in a spiritual or energetic existence.

When together with others, energy is shared. The more time spent together, the stronger that energetic bond. When someone moves beyond the veil, there is a void left behind. Where once there was relationship, now there is emptiness to be healed.

The spirit world is right here, even though you may not always see or sense it. Think about a telephone or TV; to tune in to the frequency, you require the connection. In physical form, the vibration is a lower frequency, making it difficult to tune in to the higher vibrational frequencies of the spirit realm. The spirit realm can tune in to the physical vibration. They learn to slow down their vibration to communicate on the physical plane.

To communicate with those who have passed beyond the veil, speak to them out loud, in your mind or tune in to the emotions connected to them. They will hear you and know your thoughts. To have a two-way conversation requires learning to tune in to the higher frequency. (This ability is available to all. Upon incarnation, e generally chose to forget as a part of living in "Earth School.")

Today's worksheet is a list of ways to communicate with your loved ones who have gone beyond. Choose two and practice. Be patient with yourself as you listen and watch for signs. Remember, an athlete is not born after one visit to the gym—so give yourself time to tune in to this higher vibration.

Worksheet

4 primary channels of communication:

crown

third eye

throat

heart

solar plexus

sacrum

root

claircognicance
clear knowing — crown chakra

clairvoyance
seeing — third eye chakra

clairaudience
hearing — ear chakras

clairsentience
feeling — heart chakras

Which of these feels most natural and available to you? (You have access to all. One may be stronger than the others.) The biggest obstacle will be trying too hard, straining out of fear that you will miss a message. Relax and practice until you feel comfortable.

To develop your senses requires "changing your mind". Decide that this new type of sensing is a safe, normal practice and be patient with yourself.

CLAIRAUDIECE

LISTENING TO ALL ENHANCES AND EXPANDS RECEPTIVITY.

Exercise 1 – Write down your question on a piece of paper. Center yourself, ground and connect. Then ask the question. What is the first thing you "hear" in your head? Write it down.

CLAIRAUDIECE

LISTENING TO ALL ENHANCES AND EXPANDS RECEPTIVITY.

Exercise 2 – Write out your question. Practice listening to the thoughts and words that come to the forefront of your mind, and journal them without stopping to think, edit, or rephrase. (This is called automatic writing.)

_____

_____

_____

_____

_____

_____

_____

_____

_____

_____

_____

_____

_____

_____

CLAIRVOYANCE

THE THIRD EYE IS AVAILABLE UPON REQUEST.

Exercise 1 - Ground and connect using the practices you learned earlier. Visualize the third eye opening, and state that you are ready to see. Pose a question with physical eyes closed, and "see" the answer in your minds' eye. Then, write it down here.

CLAIRVOYANCE

THE THIRD EYE IS AVAILABLE UPON REQUEST.

Exercise 2 —Pick an upcoming event. State that you are ready to "see" how the event will unfold and any details small or large. Write down your visualizations. Review them after the event.

CLAIRSENTENANCE

AN OPEN HEART IS A RECEIVING HEART.

Exercise 1 - Begin to notice the feelings that surface as you transition from one room to another and one location to another. Write about the differences.

CLAIRSENTENANCE

AN OPEN HEART IS A RECEIVING HEART.

Exercise 2- Note the feelings that arise when you are with one person verses another. Notice the shifts in energy and mood you experience.

CLAIRCOGNICANCE

THE CROWN CHAKRA IS THE ENTRYWAY OF SPIRIT CONNECTION.

Exercise 1 – Connect to you higher self / Angels / Guides / Source. Pick a topic that you would like information about. Ask the question, paying particular attention to the flow of information streaming in and your "gut feelings" from moment to moment. You will sense a settling and an understanding surrounding the topic or scenario. Journal your answers.

CLAIRCOGNICANCE

THE CROWN CHAKRA IS THE ENTRYWAY OF SPIRIT CONNECTION.

Exercise 2 – Prior to meeting someone or going somewhere, tap in to what you "know" about that person or how the room will feel, the conversations and moods. Use your first thought, not allowing your head (ego self) to interfere. Journal your thoughts, then compare them to your experience.

_____

_____

_____

_____

_____

_____

_____

_____

_____

_____

_____

_____

_____

_____

ADDITIONAL NOTES

DAY TWENTY-NINE

The Heart

DAY TWENTY-NINE

The Heart

Affirmation:

"On this day, my heart is fully open to giving and receiving love."

This is what you are working toward: opening your heart, giving love and receiving love.

As discussed on day 26, the heart is the middle energy center and sends love in all directions, nourishing the soul. This is not the physical heart, which provides for the whole physical body. It is the spiritual, energetic heart.

The heart center is known as your fourth chakra. Chakras are spinning energy wheels and are a part of your life force. They connect you to your Higher Self, Creation, God and/or Universe, and are part of what makes you unique. The heart chakra is the key to greater love in your life. It is the gateway to divine love.

Today is a guided meditation. This meditation dives deep into the heart, fully opening and connecting to yourself and to God, and is infused with a heart blessing. Allow yourself at least 30 minutes to work with this meditation.

Today's worksheet is for you to take notes and reflect on your meditation time. Have it nearby before starting the meditation or have your notebook ready.

Find a quiet place to sit comfortably for this visualization session. Make sure you will not be disturbed. Engage with the audio recording* or guide yourself through this reflection.

---

*You can download an audio version of this guided meditation at https://thesoulsharmony.com/40-Day-Soul-Expansion-Download/

Meditation

Heart Blessing Meditation

Close your eyes. Bring your awareness to your breath.

Breathe in through your nose and out through your mouth. In, out. In, out…

Bring your breath below your sacral (second) chakra and into your root (first) chakra. In, out, dropping the breath deeper and deeper …

Focus on your inner life light, usually located near your belly button. See the universal light within you expand with each breath, growing bigger and bigger, completely surrounding your physical body. See the light in front of you, behind you, above and below you. See it to the left and to the right—a complete bubble of light encasing you, holding you safely in your space.

Once again, locating the central spark of your life light, follow it as it travels down below your root chakra, down through the ground. Down, down, all the way into Gaia or Mother Earth, meeting, joining in union. Feel the strength of Gaia's love and grounding.

Focusing once again on your center spark of life-light, follow the stream upward, through your heart, your throat, your third eye, your crown and into the galactic. See the galaxies and stars around you. Now continue to follow this stream of light beyond the universe, into the nothingness—the still, calm Oneness of Source, God. See your light suspended in this blissful, universal expansion of total acceptance. Feel your ribbon of light flow gracefully in this Oneness.

Notice your feelings and emotions as you share freely and openheartedly in the bliss of the All. What color or colors do you reflect? Accept your beauty, your connection and the love, support and blessings awaiting you here. Know that there is no separation. All is One. One is All.

(Receiving of the Blessing)

Begin to move back into the cosmos, sending out heartfelt gratitude for this reminder of your true self and bringing with you the love, support and blessings received. Slowly follow your light back down toward your crown, down, down, streaming in through the top of your head, past your third eye, throat and heart, and returning to your core self. Breathe in the fullness of your true self. Know your worth. Feel your expansion. Own your blessings.

Count down from three. When you come to one, you will be completely back in the room and back in your body.

Three: becoming aware of the room and the space around you.

Two: your body is awakening. Feel your fingers and your toes begin to wriggle. Take deep breaths in and out.

One: when you are ready, open your eyes.

Worksheet

Heart Blessing Meditation

What color/colors was your ribbon of light?

What feelings/emotions did you experience in the bliss?

What was your level of Oneness with God/Source?

In the quiet, what was your heart experience?

_____

_____

_____

_____

_____

Do you feel a shift within your heart? Note any differences.

_____

_____

_____

_____

_____

What blessings did you experience?

_____

_____

_____

_____

_____

What was your overall experience in the bliss?

_____

_____

_____

_____

_____

_____

_____

_____

_____

_____

_____

_____

Choose one adjective to describe your meditative experience.

_____

Use this meditation regularly to lift, connect, and find your blessings.

DAY THIRTY

The Healer Within

Affirmation:

"On this day, I align my inner healer with pure cosmic healing frequencies."

Many search for healing from outside sources, looking to fulfill this need through a partner, family and friends. Counselors, books or even courses like the one you are doing right now are used. These are all excellent sources that assist with and stimulate your knowing. Real healing is only found within.

You are able to heal yourself. It is a choice. For healing to be fully infused in the soul and in life, a spark in the heart is required. Once you find love for yourself, you begin to grow and share that love. It naturally flows out as a part of your persona, your imprint—and it heals everything it touches.

How do you find the healer within? Start by calming the ego.

The ego "thinks" that it is in control. It runs rampant, spitting out all kinds of silly thoughts and "what if" scenarios. It drags you into the past and fills you with drama talk, all in the name of distraction. If you stay distracted, it (the ego) keeps its status as the leader. Where is the peace and calm in that mess?

The ego-mind is powerful, sneaky and self-serving. However, you can learn to harness it and use it as a resource, instead of allowing it to use you as a platform. Such a "flip" is not easy. There is no overnight fix, no pill to take to remedy the problem. It will take focus, dedication, patience and lots and lots of self-love to leash the ego and start living from your heart.

The heart knows its worth. It knows you can lasso the ego and use the mind as a tool of the heart. Focus on this new way of being as the end result—the light at the end of the tunnel.

Practice being in the Now. This brings the mind into the present and squeezes out the chatter. One way to practice this is to "see" with your mind's eye every word that is being spoken to you and every word you speak. This will slow down your thoughts and your speech, and keep the mind occupied and focused in the moment. If you are a fast talker, begin to breathe in between your words instead of letting the mind run wild and your thoughts spill out through your mouth.

Another way to practice presence is to choose a word to use to bring your focus back when you find your mind drifting, taking you into fictitious conversations, dwelling on what-ifs or making lists of things you would rather be doing. For example, every time you find your thoughts wandering, think the word "NOW." Picture the word NOW in capital letters in your mind's eye. This is a reminder to put the ego back in its place and bring your attention back to the present.

Detach from the ego. When thinking or talking about the ego, avoid using the words, "my mind" or "my ego". Disown it. Replace the word "my" with "the", saying "the mind" or "the ego". This will begin the process of realizing that "it" is not "you". It is only a part of you that you can access when you need it.

Meditation is another highly effective avenue to quiet the mind. When you first start out, shutting off the ticker-tape of thoughts can seem impossible—keep practicing. Start with a few minutes, two or three times a day, then lengthen the time as you progress. Do not get discouraged: the mind sneaks in even for seasoned practitioners.

These simple practices will set you in motion toward a physically, mentally, emotionally and soulfully balanced and healed life!

Worksheet

Below are some practices to gain control of the ego. Begin to incorporate them into your daily life. The sooner you put the ego in check, the sooner you connect to your true self and clear space for your higher self to guide you.

1. In your mind's eye, "see" each word spoken to you. Also, "see" the words you speak. This will assist with focusing and living in the moment. *

2. If you are a fast talker, take time to pause and breathe between your thoughts and sentences. This will slow your speech and assist with speaking with clarity and purpose.

3. Choose a word that brings you back into the moment when you find the mind wandering—for example, the word "NOW." Picture your word in capital letters. This practice shifts your thoughts away from the distraction.

MY WORD: _____

4. Detach from the ego by changing the words "my mind" or "my ego" to "the mind" or "the ego". By disowning the ego, it is easier to notice when it distracts you.

5. Begin a meditation practice. Start with 3-5 minutes, 2-3 times per day. As you practice, begin to lengthen the time. This practice teaches mind control in small doses to assist with strength and duration.

Soon, you will find balance in all four quadrants, Physical, Spiritual/Energetic, Mental, and Emotional!

---

*This content is, in part, adapted from conversations with my Life Coach, Dr. Carol McCall, PhD, MCC, Founder, of The Institute for Global Listening and Communication, LLC. You can learn more about Dr. Carol at www.listeningprofitsu.com.

DAY THIRTY-ONE

Honoring Self

Affirmation:

"On this day, I claim my self-worth and project it throughout my persona."

Completely honoring your self means finding your core truths, owning them and pairing them up to create the "me" you truly are.

You have discovered outside influences which began at birth and will continue to contribute until you consciously choose to stop them. You have discovered how to discern the difference between your thoughts, morals and values versus the ones that you took on from others, and worked to start separating yourself from the ones that are not yours.

Now, you are going to bring in the microscope, a flashlight and a pair of tweezers, and pull out your core values, the blueprint of your soul.

You are born with your natural design. This blueprint is what makes you unique.

Every day, every moment, every thought, conversation and experience add a layer to your original design. It is like an onion and you are peeling back those sticky, smelly layers one at a time.

Your blueprint is a guidepost used to align your life purpose with the life you are living. The Life Purpose Statement you will create today is the foundation for your action plan to shift into living your purpose joyfully and in full awareness.

On your worksheet for today, you will find questions to prompt your thoughts. Keep it simple, so as to leave less room for doubt or confusion. This is a self-examination. To avoid influence, no examples will be given. Complete the first four questions on the worksheet only. When you are done, review each question and choose the one word that stands out to you most from each answer. Write the four words in the space provided on your worksheet. Use these words to create a statement that aligns with your heart.

Worksheet

Question #1 – Pick three words to describe what others are looking for when they come to you for help or advice.*

_____   _____   _____

Question #2 – What activity or activities bring you the most joy and fulfillment?

_____

_____

_____

_____

Question #3 – Time yourself. In 2 minutes, write down every descriptive word that you see as your strength

_____

_____

_____

_____

_____

_____

_____

_____

_____

Question #4 – If you had a genie in a lamp offering you one wish to use on behalf of all mankind, what would you ask for?

_____

_____

_____

Now, choose 1 word from each question above that stands out the most for you.

Q1 _____   Q2 _____

Q3 _____   Q4 _____

Using these core truths, create a statement that aligns with your heart.

My life purpose is to

_____

_____

_____

_____

_____

_____

_____

_____

_____

_____

_____

_____

_____

_____

_____

_____

_____

_____

_____

_____

Now that you have your statement, you are ready to apply this truth to your life and live with purpose!

For example, if the words from the first four questions were Reassurance, Energy Work, Inspiration and Hope, the Life Purpose Statement may be: "My life purpose is to reassure myself and others that we are worthy, through hope, inspiration and energy work."

Use your statement as an affirmation to reassure yourself that you are aligned with your original blueprint. Create your statement, own it and live it, starting today!

This content is, in part, adapted from conversations with my Life Coach, Dr. Carol McCall, PhD, MCC, Founder, of The Institute for Global Listening and Communication, LLC. You can learn more about Dr. Carol at www.listeningprofitsu.com.

226

DAY THIRTY-TWO

Focus

Affirmation:

"On this day, I step into my true self and align my future with my truths."

Yesterday, you found your life purpose and arranged it into a personal statement. This is a working tool for today's topic, "Focus".

Write out your Life Purpose Statement once again on the top of today's worksheet. In fact, write it out and post it in multiple places as a reminder. Put it in your car, on the refrigerator, on your nightstand and on the bathroom mirror. You can even write it on an index card and carry it in your pocket. Keep your Life Purpose Statement in the forefront of your thoughts. This is your purpose; you will begin to blend it into you daily life.

Take a closer look at your Life Purpose Statement and break it down into actions. The worksheet will prompt you to zero in on the action part of living with purpose. It may be infused into your current lifestyle already. You may find that you are already on the right track. You may make a few adjustments or possibly a complete flip to get back on track.

Look back at your answer to yesterday's question #4. "If you had a genie in a lamp offering you one wish for all mankind, what would you ask for?"

Are you already contributing to this dream for mankind? It can start with one person. Find ways to incorporate action into your daily activities that puts energy toward fulfilling this wish. It may only take a few minutes per day.

Look at yesterday's question #2. "What activity or activities bring you the most joy and fulfillment?" Place your answers next to your Life Purpose Statement. How can you work these into your daily life while fulfilling your life purpose?

Look for connections between your life purpose, your joy and your wish for mankind. Bring these three into alignment and you will find harmony in life.

Worksheet

My life purpose is to

_____

_____

_____

_____

_____

_____

_____

_____

_____

Post your Life Purpose Statement in multiple places (car, refrigerator, bathroom mirror, nightstand, your pocket).

Break your statement down into sections by selecting the key words that were the basis you used from yesterday's worksheet.

What role/roles do you hold within your family (matriarch, bridge, savior, etc.)?

_____

_____

_____

_____

What is your profession? _____

In your group of friends, which one are you? (select any combination of these)?

○ RESPONSIBLE   ○ FUNNY   ○ ADVENTUROUS   ○ COORDINATOR   ○ FIXER   ○ CREATIVE

○ OTHER _____

_____

_____

What are your hobbies?

_____

_____

_____

_____

What are your interests?

_____

_____

_____

_____

If you could choose your career, what would it be?

What secret passion do you have (music, acting, writing, investigation, etc.)?

Do you find one or more of your key words active and alive in your answers? If you do, you are walking a path of purpose. If not, you may look to adjust to align with your life's passion.

DAY THIRTY-THREE

Life Review

Affirmation:

"On this day, my true self and open-heart guide me to my next chapter in life."

Life is filled with highs and lows, the memories you have created over time. In this Life Review, you will use segments again. Look for patterns of open-heartedness and breathe in the joy from these memories individually and collectively.

Find a quiet place to sit comfortably for this visualization session. Make sure you will not be disturbed. Engage with the audio recording* or guide yourself through this reflection.

*You can download an audio version of this guided meditation at https://thesoulsharmony.com/40-Day-Soul-Expansion-Download/

Meditation

Life Review Meditation

Close your eyes and begin to regulate your breathing. Calm your thoughts, relax your body. Breathe deep into your abdomen, take slow, relaxing breaths.

Now, in your mind's eye, see yourself in your earliest and happiest childhood memory. Becoming fully present, look closely: do you see others there? What do they look like? As you look around, what else do you see? Are you indoors or outdoors? Look closely at the details and colors around you. What sounds do you hear? What aroma is in the air?

Now look at your child self. What do you look like? Are you sitting, standing or being held? Focusing now on the heart center of your child self, see a two-way stream of soft, pink light beaming from your heart to the heart of your child self. Feel the emotion and the love flowing to and from these two versions of self.

Closing the energy stream now, move away from this memory. Bring your awareness to your late teenage years. Scan your memories and choose the happiest memory that stands out. Now, go there. You are there now. Feel the space—are you alone or with others? What activity is going on around you? What environment are you in? Look around, taking in the whole scene. Hear the sounds.

Focusing on your teenage self, look closely. See your youthful self, vibrant, alive and carefree. Look at your hairstyle, your clothes, your shoes, your skin. Now, see the two-way stream of soft, pink light flowing from your heart to the heart of your youthful self. Feel the emotion, share the love.

Disconnect now and move back from this memory, floating further and further away. In your mind's eye, scan your memories and select your most joyful early adult memory. Choose the one that stands out the most. With just a quick thought, take yourself there, be in that memory. What do you see? What is your environment? What do you see around you? Are there other people there? What are they doing? What are they wearing? Can you hear their voices?

Bring your focus now to your young adult self. Who do you see? What are the dreams and aspirations of your young adult self? Once again, see the beautiful, soft, pink stream of light connecting your heart to the heart of your young adult self. Feel the flow of love. Send your wisdom to your youthful self and feel the flow of inspiration into your heart, sharing and receiving.

Close off this portal of light now, step back and move away from this memory.

You are back to your current self, fully present, eyes closed. Now, separate yourself into two parts. With your spiritual eyes, scan the image of yourself before you. What strengths do you recognize? What characteristics? Opening your heart now, see the stream of soft, pink light as it flows from yourself to yourself, allowing you to share with, nurture and love yourself freely. This stream of light carries with it the joy of your childhood, the vibrancy of your teenage self and the aspirations and inspiration of your young adult self. Absorb these energies, these memories. They are you. You are one.

You are merging back together with yourself now through your connecting heart portal, bringing with you all of these aspects of self. All of the joy and love is being infused into one you—full of life, full of love, full of self. Bring your awareness back now into your body. Feel joy-filled and vibrant. Begin to move about, stretching your arms, feeling carefree. Open your eyes, fully present and back in your body. You are refreshed, renewed and complete.

Worksheet

Journal your experience of each of the four versions of yourself.

CHILD SELF:

_____

_____

_____

_____

_____

_____

YOUTHFUL/TEENAGE SELF:

_____

_____

_____

_____

_____

_____

YOUNG ADULT SELF:

_____

_____

_____

_____

_____

_____

_____

CURRENT SELF:

_____

_____

_____

_____

_____

_____

What do you believe to be the gifts received from each version of self that create the "me" you are right now?

DAY THIRTY-FOUR

Living in the Now

Affirmation:

"On this day, I am present in every moment."

To live fully present requires training. Where can this training be found? Where do you sign up and get started? The truth is, it is a self-taught program. It is a lifelong commitment and the price is self-love. Make the decision to love yourself enough to gift yourself with your own life. Living in the past, thinking thoughts of "what if", replaying events over and over in the mind; these things rob you of your Now. Why would you weigh yourself down rehashing something that is never going to change? You have lived that experience, learned that lesson. Now, tuck it under the hat and move on.

Then, there is the future. What needs to be done later today, this week, this year? What deadlines need to be met for your life plan? Where are you going? These are all of importance; life is not a fairy tale where all things wonderful magically appear. How do you deal with all of life's pressures and stay present? Write it down. Keep an agenda. You have practiced segmenting your time; you already know how to arrange your time to meet your needs. Anytime you feel overwhelmed, pause, write the thoughts down using today's worksheet (which gets them out of your head), then address them during the time you have segmented for that purpose. After you write them down, bring yourself back into your Now.

As an example, being a grandparent is different than being a parent. Grandparents experience their grandchildren's "firsts" differently: first word, first step, first report card, watching their personality develop. As a grandparent witnessing the joy of these "firsts", it is easier to realize that, as parents, most of those earlier years are spent fretting over past and future, missing out on many of the important, personal moments with children. Those years have passed. The parent did the best they could at the time with the knowledge they had, so it is okay—it is the past. Worrying about missed moments of yesterday, steals away the Now.

Forfeiting this very moment to the past or the future is a form of "dying to self". As you move into the next moment, that last moment is gone. It has become the past. Are you going to relive it and let it steal your Now, too?

Moments, hours, days and weeks turn into years with a blink of the eye. Youth feels like you have your whole life ahead of you and plenty of time. Time moves so very quickly. Take advantage of the present. Align with the conversations, treasure the relationships you are experiencing with yourself and others, and fully feel the joy of the moment you are in. Chose to embrace the opportunity to be who you are, where you are, right now, in this moment.

Worksheet

You are not listing your past worries. Do you know why? They are the past, and there is nothing you can do to change them. You are FREE from them!

FUTURE RESPONSIBILITIES:

IMMEDIATE:

THIS WEEK:

THIS MONTH:

MY SHORT-TERM GOAL:

_____
_____
_____
_____
_____

ACTION NEEDED TO MAKE IT HAPPEN FOR ME	START DATE	COMPLETION DATE

MY LONG-TERM GOAL:

_____

_____

_____

_____

_____

ACTION NEEDED TO MAKE IT HAPPEN FOR ME	START DATE	COMPLETION DATE

This action sheet will start you on the track of releasing your thoughts on to paper. Transfer these committed dates on to your personal agenda. Place reminders along the way in the notes section.

DAY THIRTY-FIVE

Patience

Affirmation:

"On this day, I accept self-love and honor my progress."

Yesterday, you practiced leaving behind past thoughts and emptying tomorrows' thoughts and responsibilities out of your head and onto a piece of paper until the time you allot to address them. That leaves you in your Now, where you are at your fullest potential, living in full expression and awareness.

Wait … Is it still happening? Is it happening right now? Did your thoughts stray?

How long did it take you to get to this moment? Twenty, forty, even seventy years? It would be a miraculous achievement to completely shift away from all those years of learned behaviors simply by completing these few worksheets. (If you have mastered this already, you are depriving all of us by not sharing your secret!)

It is hard to remember all these new ways of dealing with and handling life. To create change, to live authentically, the practice of patience with yourself is required. In the last thirty-five days, you have discovered many avenues of change. You have uncovered many aspects of yourself; you have connected, disconnected and brought out the hidden truths of who you truly are. Right now, give yourself the recognition and praise you deserve for the work you have done. This is a self-development program. It is self-paced. You are self-motivated. You have worked through so much already and you have done this out of self-love.

Today, practice patience with yourself. Spend time in prayer and meditation, allowing yourself space to absorb and readjust into the fresh, new you that you have discovered.

Patience is a learned discipline. You are a teacher. You are a student of self. You are a student of life.

Practicing patience with self and others teaches you to honor yourself and others in the space you hold. It simplifies life, clears away thoughts of anxiety and judgement, and brings you in to the present moment.

Find patience by practicing patience. Align yourself in your Now, for that is where patience is. There is no past or future in the Now. There is only this moment—and in this moment there is patience, love, and experience.

Worksheet

"Patience is a virtue"

PATIENCE = the ability to accept without upset

VIRTUE = behavior showing high moral standards

LIST THE AREAS TO BEGIN PRACTICING MORE PATIENCE:

WITH SELF:

WITH OTHERS:

Below, list the action you plan to take to make this a reality for yourself. This time there is space for a date you plan to start each. Check them off as you find you have accomplished your goal.

DATE	WITH SELF	WITH OTHERS

ADDITIONAL NOTES

DAY THIRTY-SIX

Spirit Connection

Affirmation:

"On this day, I remain openly connected to my higher guidance."

There are different spirit realms or spirit worlds. The Astral Plane is where you are now and where you are when you leave the physical. Similar, yet different; it is reality as you feel it to be. You expand and grow on this plane. You attract those who vibrate at the same frequency.

The Thought Plane or Ethereal World is a higher vibration. There is no up or down, above or below, only different frequencies. An earlier comparison was to our radios, telephones and televisions, which must have a connection to "tune in". The Ethereal World is the plane of pure thought, where inspirational thoughts are originated and sent to the Astral Plane. The Ethereal World is the point of purity of mind and thought. The teachings of Abraham from Ester Hicks, The Law of Attraction, and A Course in Miracles by Jane Roberts are channeled from this realm, which is also home to your higher self where you find wisdom, ideas and inspiration. Souls are not limited here and it is not controlled by space or time. It is all thought.

The Celestial or Angelic Realm is also known as the Bliss Realm. Only divine love and joy exist here. All are of one consciousness; there is no division. This level of consciousness asks for nothing and its only existence is pure love, the energy of the universe. This Realm is home to those who are highly elevated spiritually: angels, archangels, masters and prophets. These souls act as conduits, transmitting God's love to other realms. Most of the souls in the Celestial realm have never walked the Earth, except for a few like Jesus, Moses, Elijah, Enoch and Buddha. These souls are connected to all life; their radiance is bright and full. They have reached the path to love, yet, still evolving, they give love to all who ask.

You are all able to connect to any and all levels of consciousness to ask for guidance. During your meditation time, focus on connecting to each level of consciousness. Note the way you feel when connected, the clarity of your messages and the feelings or emotions stimulated in you. When you are finished, use discernment to determine whether the connection you are making is from a pure light source and therefore aligned with your higher good.

Worksheet

The
Astral
World

The
Ethereal
World

The
Celestial
Realm

THE ASTRAL WORLD – Where you are now and where you go when you transition. It is reality as you feel it to be. You expand and grow on this plane. You attract those who vibrate at the same frequency.

THE ETHEREAL WORLD (aka the Thought Plane) – Inspirational thoughts are originated and sent to the Astral Plane. Your higher self-resides here. Souls are not limited and can divide consciousness.

THE CELESTIAL REALM (aka the Angelic Realm) – Angels, Archangels, Masters and prophets send God's love to other realms and send blessings and gifts of guidance and knowledge to the Astral Plane. The Bliss Level. Pure Oneness. No division; all are of one consciousness. The energy of the Universe.

Practice connecting to each plane during meditation.

How did your connection feel?

_____

_____

_____

_____

_____

_____

_____

_____

_____

Did you receive a message?

What level of clarity did you discern?

What feelings/emotions were stimulated?

_____

_____

_____

_____

_____

_____

_____

You can test the spirits as often as you want by asking for their origin. Uplifting feelings are higher frequencies. Heavy, dense or anxious feelings are lower frequencies. Only the lower energy forms get irritated. Higher vibrational beings have patience.

ADDITIONAL NOTES

260

DAY THIRTY-SEVEN

Spiritual Sight

Affirmation:

"On this day, I am open to receiving clarity through spiritual vision."

There are four channels of spiritual connection called the "Four Clairs":

CLAIRSENTIENCE (clear feeling)
CLAIRAUDIENCE (clear hearing)
CLAIRCOGNIZANCE (clear knowing)
CLAIRVOYANCE (clear seeing)

"Spiritual sight" or clairvoyance is the ability to "see" with the third eye, located just above and between the physical eyes. All have the ability to see with the third eye—it is up to you to decide whether you want to or not. Some have a heightened awareness of this ability and some will require practice and exercise to strengthen the connection.

To become aware of your third eye, ground yourself, as in our previous meditations, by sending your heart light down to core earth. Then, follow the light back up, through your heart and out through your crown to connect to the universal God light. Once you are aligned with the energies, bring your awareness to your third eye. It looks like a physical eye. Open the lid. Now you are ready to do your practices.

Today's worksheet is a suggested list of practices to assist in the development of clairvoyance.

To develop clairvoyance, release all fears, be open to receiving and use your visualization and imagination to "see" a visual image with the mind's eye. You may ask and look for images and specifics about the spirit or event. You may ask for memories, such as a death scene or a scene from childhood. Ask for details like colors, smells and environment. You can even ask for a picture or a scene in the future. If it is blurry or not close enough for you to see, ask for the image to be clearer or closer.

Accessing your third eye does not mean it has to be open all the time. When you do not want to "see", visualize closing the lid to your third eye. It is a good practice to keep your eye open at selective times, be aware of and particular about what, when and where you want to receive. Be sure you are fully grounded and connected to pure universal light before *any* practice.

Worksheet

Use the practice above to open your third eye and connect to Universal/God energy.

Telepathically send out a request to "see" a scene of an event you are scheduled to attend (ex: a lunch date, work meeting, etc.) Place yourself in that scene. Ask to see specifics about the event: who else is there, what are the surroundings, look for details (clothes, scents, emotions).

Write down the details, then, during and after the event, note the similarities from your vision. Remember, this takes practice!

---

* *The information in this worksheet is based on information shared in James Van Praagh's "Psychic Portals" Course, Lesson #1 "Clairvoyaance," Session:"Pop Up"*

Think of a question–for example, "What will my relationship/family status look like in two years?" or "What will my career look like a year from today?" Now, focusing on your question and using a focal object of your choice (such as the flame of a candle, a pendulum, or a similar item), unfocus your eyes, stare into the object, and relax the mind as you travel in to the time and event requested. Ask your question, ask for details, and pay attention to what you see. When you are done, write down your first thoughts.

NOTE: Trying too hard will block your connection. Relax and have fun with this!

Choose a space in your home, inside or outside. Sit quietly. Choose an object to connect with. Become the object. See the world from the perspective of that object. What do you see, and from what angle? What is your purpose? Your shape? How does it feel to be this object?

Practice shifting your energy from yourself to the object and back. This is a visualization practice that you can do with practically any object.

ADDITIONAL NOTES

DAY THIRTY-EIGHT

Healing Intentions

Affirmation:

"On this day, I will purposefully align with my true self."

Today is a discovery meditation. Once you have completed the meditation (with the audio or without), have your worksheet available for journaling your experience.

Note: if you are using the audio, be aware that we will have two points of silence in this meditation. This will be your time to just "be" in the moment. The audio will resume automatically. Relax and take in the beauty and vision around you.

Find a quiet place to sit comfortably for this visualization session. Make sure you will not be disturbed. Begin to regulate your breath and calm your mind and body. Engage with the audio recording* or guide yourself through this reflection.

*You can download an audio version of this guided meditation at https://thesoulsharmony.com/40-Day-Soul-Expansion-Download/

Meditation

Healing Meditation

See yourself standing in the sun. Ahead of you is a field of tall grass. As you walk toward the field, you see a small path. Follow the path into the field.

The sun is high and bright. Feel the gentle breeze blowing on your face. Listen as the birds sing in the distance. As you walk down the path, notice that there are butterflies floating all around you–hundreds of them everywhere. They follow you through the field. Feel their carefree beauty as you float along the pathway.

The singing of the birds gets a bit louder as you come upon a clearing. Standing in the clearing is a huge ancient oak tree. Approach the tree and reach out to touch the bark, feeling the strength of the oak. Under the tree you see a quilt–a family heirloom, battered and torn from years of use. Lay down on the quilt. Feel the love, warmth and comfort the quilt holds for you.

Relaxing under the tree, feel the earth beneath you, grounding you and pulling away any stress, worries or concerns, taking it all away and drawing it into the earth. Feel the breeze on your skin. Notice the sun's rays as they peek through the top of the oak tree. See the leaves and branches sway and hear the birds sing.

Now, close your eyes. Find an even deeper relaxation, comfort and love in this space. You are safe in this space. Now, ask yourself, "What do I need to release and heal for my highest and greatest good at this time?" Relax in this safe, loving space and feel the impressions and answers as they flow freely in and around you.

Sit in silence for about 3-5 minutes to receive the answers to this question.

As you note of your answers, send your gratitude and love to your guides, angels and God for bringing you the guidance and blessings to clear and heal as you move through this lesson. Picture yourself releasing these energies and patterns. Watch as they float up, away from you, no longer a part of your life and no longer allowed to share your space. See pure love and light replace these old patterns and fill the space now. Feel the newfound joy in your soul.

Pause for 2-3 minutes to allow yourself to feel the new joy.

As you lay under the tree on the quilt, picture yourself slowly opening your eyes, still feeling the gentle breeze, hearing the birds sing and seeing the sun's rays peeking through the trees. Picture yourself standing up, still feeling the love and joy in your soul and knowing that you are healed and free.

Begin your walk back down the path through the field of tall grass. The butterflies are floating all around you and you feel as light and carefree as the butterflies. As you come back to the clearing, notice the butterflies again in their abundance. What color or colors are they?

Then, walk away from the grassy field and become aware of your body again. Bring your awareness back into the room and slowly move or stretch. Take a few deep breaths and open your eyes when you are ready.

Worksheet

Healing Meditation Notes

WHAT COLOR WERE YOUR BUTTERFLIES? _____

The color/colors of the butterflies in your experience are related to the areas of healing and release.

RED – Root/Base Chakra-finances/career/home/physical safety and needs

ORANGE – Sacral Chakra-creativity/reproduction/sexuality

YELLOW – Solar Plexus Chakra-claircognizance/personal power/digestion

GREEN – Heart Chakra-clairsentience/heart health/life purpose/love

BLUE – Throat Chakra-communication/truth/speaking up/healing messages

RED VIOLET – Ear Chakras-clairaudient/negative self-talk/verbal abuse

INDIGO – Third Eye Chakra-clairvoyance/higher self-connection/self-truth

VIOLET – Crown Chakra-divine guidance connection

NOTES

What messages did you receive from your question, "What do I need to release and heal for my highest and greatest good at this time?"

_____

_____

_____

_____

_____

_____

_____

_____

What was your connection? (Higher Self, Angels, Guides, God, Archangels, etc.)

_____

_____

_____

_____

_____

_____

_____

What energies did you release and heal?

Write an affirmation, confirming your healing/release and infusing this space with pure love and light.

DAY THIRTY-NINE

Faith & Reflection of God

Affirmation:

"On this day, I have faith that I am of value in this world."

On Day 16, "Gods' Promise", you practiced recognition of faith. Every step of your path has been infused with light, love and support. You have discovered the spirit realms, peeled back the layers of blindness, relinquished distractions and cleared the path to your true self—your blueprint. The unveiling of truths, heighten awareness of self and make accessible the space inside where God is reflected and faith is found.

Today, you will meet your Guardian Angel and other guides, and begin to familiarize yourself with the energies and characteristics of each. As with all of the meditations, you will benefit from revisiting this one as many times as you are called; each repetition will deepen your connection and give you greater clarity around the guidance and messages you receive every day. The more faith you have in your ability to receive these messages, the more powerfully you will receive them.

Before beginning the meditation, think about any questions you may have for your guides. Once again, have your worksheet nearby, and, if you choose to engage with the audio, wait to start the meditation until you are in a special, quiet space. Begin to regulate the breath and calm the mind and body. Then begin your meditation. Find a quiet place to sit comfortably for this visualization session. Make sure you will not be disturbed. Engage with the audio recording* or guide yourself through this reflection.

---

*You can download an audio version of this guided meditation at https://thesoulsharmony.com/40-Day-Soul-Expansion-Download/

Meditation

Faith & Reflection of God Meditation

Picture yourself by the ocean. Notice the abundance of water. Hear the waves, feel the warm breeze, hear the birds as they float freely in the wind. Feel your skin tingling as the sun warms you.

Walk toward the shoreline. Feel the cool waves on your bare feet. Raising your face toward the sky, see a soft, white, fluffy cloud floating toward you. Reach out and touch the cloud. Feel its soft, welcoming energy. Step up on to the cloud and melt into the safe comfort of its gentleness. As your cloud rises higher into the sky, feel your weightlessness. Feel your body becoming lighter and lighter as you float into the love of all that is. Notice how your body feels. Notice the subtle way your thoughts flow as you become one with the cloud.

As you float, carefree, notice another cloud approaching. As it comes closer, you will feel a familiar energy— kind, loving, angelic. This is your Guardian Angel. Can you see a face or an image? Do you feel an impression or emotion in this energy? What colors are present?

Relaxing into the oneness that you share, accept the hand of your Guardian and step onto the cloud.

Looking up, you will see a staircase forming in front of you. Guided safely by your guardian, begin to ascend the staircase. With each step, feel safer, lighter, loved.

Continue moving up the stairs. When you reach the top, notice a grand table before you. Around this table, you will see images which seem familiar, illuminated by pure, golden light. Their energies emit kindness, compassion and pure love for you, and you know that they are gathered together in celebration of you and your life, eager to guide and assist you in every way.

Approach the table. Feel the love bond between yourself and each soul at the table. Are there any familiar energies or faces? Do you feel closer to one in particular or are you equally drawn to all? Begin connecting with each individually, one at a time, sensing the uniqueness of the connection and noting your feelings and impressions from each.

Once you have made a connection with each, invite them to visit with you often, and send your love and gratitude for their kinship and dedication to you.

Taking your Guardian's hand, begin to descend the staircase, carrying in your heart the abundance of love you have experienced in your circle of guides. This love will be forever in your heart.

Step back onto the cloud, once again connecting with and trusting your Guardian. Feel the eternal bond between you and know that you are completely and forever as one in love.

As the cloud floats back toward the ocean's edge, notice the familiar sounds of the birds. Feel the breeze and the suns warmth. As you step back into the waves, feel the coolness on your feet.

As you walk away from the shoreline, become aware of your surroundings. Bring your awareness back into the room, taking slow, deep breaths, integrating slowly back into the Now. Slowly move or stretch your body and open your eyes when you are ready.

Take notes on your thoughts, impressions and experiences, colors you have noticed, and any messages you received from your visit with your guides.

Worksheet

Healing Meditation Notes

MY QUESTION FOR MY GUIDES:

_____

_____

_____

_____

_____

What did you experience with you Guardian Angel (the escort on the cloud and the stairway)?

_____

_____

_____

_____

_____

_____

Describe your Guardian Angel in as much detail as you can.

_____

_____

_____

_____

_____

_____

_____

What energies did you sense at the table? How many?

_____

_____

_____

_____

_____

_____

_____

What images/impressions did you receive?

If you brought a question to your guides, did you feel an answer, inspiration or guidance surrounding the topic?

Describe your overall experience at the table.

What was your impression of your presence?

ADDITIONAL NOTES

DAY FORTY

Reflections of Lessons

Affirmation:

*On this day, I fully identify with my ever-expanding awareness,
and embrace continued growth."*

The creation of this workbook has been an eye-opening, love-lifting journey for me. I pray that you are feeling the same joy, expansion and alignment as I am in this moment. Spirit has guided us through these days together, enlightening us with knowledge, truth, understanding and the blessings of Oneness.

This in-depth program has challenged you in all four quadrants: physical, mental, emotional and spiritual.

The journaling and worksheets you have compiled in this workbook and your notebook will serve you well as you continue on your path of self-discovery. You can return to your favorite exercises over and over, as often as you like, so that you always feel centered in your joy and connected to the Oneness of life and God/Universe. As you write each new chapter of your play, entitled "My Life", review your previous notes and worksheets to compare where you were previously to the elevated state you have grown in to. You will easily notice the expansion you have created in yourself.

You come into this life to seek truth and knowledge to grow your soul. Opening your heart to more fully give and receive love expands, enriches and brightens your soul light. "This is how we change the world: one drop of light at a time."

Thank you for your trust and for opening and sharing your heart with me.

Much love and many blessings on "our" journey to soul expansion.

Worksheet

Use this space to reflect on your experience over the last forty days and the lessons that were the most significant for you. Write out the soul shifts you have felt and journal your thoughts on what might be coming next as you continue your journey.

About the Author

Tearhsa Wilder is the founder of The Souls Harmony. She is an intuitive healer and spiritual guidance teacher. Tearhsa is the author of 40 Days to Soul Enlightenment and the 40 Days to Soul Enlightenment Daily Affirmation Deck.

Her gift of channeling the upper realms has led her to "The Movement of Enlightenment". The goal of The Movement of Enlightenment is to open hearts to truth and knowledge.

Tearhsa is fulfilling her life purpose as a healer of hearts through her writing, teaching and energy healing practice. This work has opened her heart and the hearts of many others, to healing, joy and self-worth. As Tearhsa shares her heart, she trusts that all who receive, find joy, worthiness and love of self.

Tearhsa lives in Myrtle Beach, South Carolina.

www.ingramcontent.com/pod-product-compliance
Lightning Source LLC
Chambersburg PA
CBHW062032090426
42733CB00035B/2615